SQUARE MILE TALES

BY

TONY DRURY

A London veteran reveals what happened to him during a forty-year career in banking and finance in the City (known as 'the Square Mile') and the rather interesting characters, several of whom were fraudsters, he met along the way – not to mention some controversial politicians.

Cover Design by Tee Rex Cover Design

ISBN: 978-1-910040-46-1

"The world is quite like London, it's not good, it's not bad, it just is. There's no morality, or dishonour, just your own lonely code, until your race is run, until the end."

These words were attributed to Reggie Kray in the 2015 film 'Legend' which traces the rise and fall of the notorious East End London gangsters, the Kray twins. From the late 1950s until 1967, Ronnie and Reggie took over organised crime, operating, often with fearsome violence, from the Mile End Road. This was one of the earliest suburbs of London and the first to be hit by a V-1 flying bomb in the Second World War, in June 1944, which killed eight people and wounded thirty.

The Krays progressed into West End nightlife and gaming clubs where they attracted the celebrities including Diana Dors, Frank Sinatra, Judy Garland and Richard Harris. Their links extended into the Houses of Parliament and the American mafia. Ronnie said that "the Beatles were the rulers of pop music, me and my brother ruled London. We were fucking untouchable."

In 1969, at the Central Criminal Court (known as the 'Old Bailey'), they were sentenced to life imprisonment following the longest murder hearing in the history of the British criminal justice system. The judge, Justice Melford Stevenson, opined, "in my view, society has earned a rest from your activities."

Ronnie (61) died in March 1995; Reggie (66) in October 2000. During his lengthy time in prison, he became a born-again Christian.

FOREWORD

Tony Drury, by professional qualification, is a Fellow of the Chartered Institute of Bankers. In these tales he recalls his career lasting over forty years from being a cashier at Midland Bank, Kidderminster, to creating his own corporate finance house based in London, at St Helen's Place, in the centre of the Square Mile, which is also known as 'the City'. Samuel Johnson, considered by many to be one of the greatest literary figures of the eighteenth century, said, "Sir, when a man is tired of London, he is tired of life; for there is in London all that life can afford."

The author relished his years in the City and now relates his personal odyssey through the financial and political events of the time and the personalities who dominated the headlines. He travelled extensively in the Far East and met a few suspicious people along the way. He mixed business with politics and came across some interesting characters.

This is an autobiography written with an emphasis on the writer's commercial and political experiences. These include his explosive time with Robert Maxwell, dinner with the controversial Conservative Member of Parliament, Nadine Dorries, his knowledge of the New Zealander who secretly photographed Diana, Princess of Wales, his boardroom meeting with the American fraudster Elizabeth Holmes, the sudden appearance at dinner of (Sir) Iain Duncan Smith and meeting with a number of prime ministers: these are just some of his experiences during a forty-plus years' career based mainly in the Square Mile.

There are further incidences including his arrest by Chinese border guards when trying to cross over from Hong Kong into Shenzhen. When on business in China he was rushed to the hospital in central Beijing hosting foreign travellers where he was treated by the caring Dr Wang.

This is, however, also a tale of relationships between a banker/corporate financier who relished his politics and the

1

extraordinary collection of people he met along the way including Ghislaine Maxwell who he once employed.

*****

Financial centres, operating the global money markets, are to be found around the world ranging from Scotland's West End in Edinburgh, the German financial centre in Frankfurt, America's Wall Street in Lower Manhattan, New York City, Hong Kong's International Financial Centre in Kowloon, the Chinese World Financial Centre in the Pudong district of Shanghai, the Central Business District in Singapore and many more.

London is a sprawling metropolis covering more than six hundred square miles. The original City of London is said to represent its beating heart and is nicknamed the 'Square Mile' in recognition of the 1.12 square miles it actually covers. The City, differentiated by the use of the capital 'C', was founded in the first century AD on the northern banks of the River Thames in the aftermath of the Roman invasion. It survived the 1605 attempt by Guy Fawkes to blow up the Houses of Parliament and the 1666 Great Fire which destroyed eighty per cent of its buildings. It saw King George II make 10 Downing Street available to Britain's first Prime Minister, Sir Robert Walpole, and survived – during the First World War – German zeppelins dropping incendiary bombs over its historic landscape.

The Square Mile contains the Bank of England, formed in 1694 to act as the English Government's banker, the London Stock Exchange created in 1801, Mansion House, the official residence of the Lord Mayor, Guildhall, in Moorgate, the ceremonial and administrative centre of the City and St Paul's, the Anglican Cathedral, which is the seat of the Bishop of London and is on Ludgate Hill, the highest point in the City.

Its domestic and securities activities dominate and it is a location for international eurocurrency business, eurobond transactions, insurance, foreign exchange, fund management and corporate financial advice. In 2018 the City of London statisticians estimated that 374,000 people worked in financial, professional and business services. The coronavirus pandemic, lockdowns and the 'working from home' culture have combined to change the picture.

For many it is still the greatest financial centre in the world. It is where Tony Drury spent much of his career during which he met some amazing people leading to memories, experiences and stories he can now reveal.

The Institute of Bankers

10 Lombard Street, London, E.C.3.
17th March, 1983.

Sir,

I have the honour to inform you that the Council have this day elected you a Fellow of The Institute of Bankers.

I am, Sir,

Yours faithfully,

Secretary-General

Mr. A.C. Drury, F.I.B.

INTRODUCTION

It is one of the corniest jokes in the comedian's repertoire:

Patient: "Doctor, am I going to die?"
Doctor: "Yes, you are. You are asking me, 'when?'"

It would seem to be a realistic assumption that many writers of autobiographies have a sense of impending closure. Some, sadly, may be aware of their personal prognosis. Writing one's own obituary has become more popular in recent times: a number of moving, even poignant examples have gone viral online. There are many sayings attributed to the famous concerning one's demise. It was Benjamin Franklin who, in 1789, said, "nothing is certain except death and taxes."

For some writers there are many years ahead: in Chapter Nine I mention that currently, according to the latest government statistics, there are 15,200 people living in the four home countries aged over one hundred years.

The responsibility of the author is to entertain their audience. It never occurred to me that my own autobiography could achieve that objective. I am one of the 67.5 million people living in the United Kingdom and, as such, have not scaled the heights to warrant the sobriquet of 'celebrity'. An associate read an article I had written about people I had met in my career and suggested this autobiography, provided it concentrated on the political, commercial and social backgrounds to each recollection. The pioneer of the American animation industry, Walt Disney, said that "growing old is mandatory, but growing up is optional." This prompts an introspective aspect in writing your own history as one reflects on situations experienced. It is doubtful that I have improved with age albeit I am clear of the warning given by the Italian writer Cesare Pavese who suggested that "the real affliction of old age is remorse."

My career took place mainly in the City (of London) or through resulting connections such as overseas company directorships. Along the way I came across a community of amazing people, some of great accomplishment, several for individual pinnacles achieved and others because they were either controversial and/or fraudsters. I did not enjoy being arrested by Chinese border guards. You now have the opportunity to decide for yourself whether 'Square Mile Tales' reflects an interesting journey.

CONTENTS

CHAPTER ONE
"WAIT FOR ME, LONDON, I'M ON MY WAY! CRISIS? WHAT CRISIS?"

It may seem unlikely but I was appointed to my Square Mile banking position when having coffee with my boss in the middle of Whipsnade Zoo, a few miles off the M1 motorway. As the general manager was telling me that I was moving from Birmingham to London, an elephant passed by the restaurant window and emitted an excess of rectal wind. Perhaps I should have heeded the warning. The year was 1973 and there was an almighty financial crash on its way.

*****

Life started with a bang as I was born on Guy Fawkes night in November 1946, in Birmingham, as part of the post-Second World War baby boomer generation. That was not the only explosion the world was experiencing. The unstable global political situation was dominated by the ideological clash between capitalism and communism which was labelled by the democratic socialist and novelist George Orwell as the 'cold war'. This manifested itself in three ways: the testing of new weapons and the threat of a nuclear war; fierce competition over allegiances with newly independent nations following the end of the Second World War; and military and economic support of strategically placed countries.

Thus, the Korean War (1950 – 53) saw the north supported by China and the Soviet Union invade the south backed by the United States and her allies. This was followed by the Cuban revolution which was to lead to the October 1962 Cuban missile crisis and further confrontation between the United States and the Soviet Union. November 1955 saw the start of the Vietnam War which concluded just under twenty years later in April 1975 with the fall of Saigon.

British attention was focused on the Middle East, and, in particular, Egypt, where, in July 1956, President Nasser nationalised the Suez Canal, a vital waterway link owned by shareholders in Britain and France and which carried two-thirds of Middle Eastern oil consumed in Europe. In October, Israeli troops invaded the Egyptian Sinai followed by British and French paratroopers who landed in an effort to secure the canal. The Egyptians sank forty ships and the waterway did not reopen until March 1957. Such was the political pressure applied by the United States and the USSR that the European troops withdrew and the Suez Crisis came to a conclusion. In January 1957, Conservative Prime Minister Anthony Eden resigned his office.

Later in 1957, political attention switched to the start of the space race with the launching by the Soviets of Sputnik 1.

At home, in Birmingham, we knew hunger and hardship: my mother, fresh from the austerity of the war years, could extract unbelievable goodness from chicken or, occasionally, beef carcasses and Sunday lunch was dominated by eating dripping on toast. I had one pair of shoes. It was not until the early nineteen fifties when food rationing eased and my father's career began to prosper that life slowly improved. He was now a Midland Bank manager and rather reminiscent of Captain Mainwaring in 'Dad's Army'. In 1954 he bought an Austin A30 car for around £500 and we had our first summer holiday in Devon which I can recall involved about eight hours of bottleneck traffic jams.

I attended King Edward's Five Ways Grammar School and loved every minute of it: Prefect, House Captain, First Team Rugby and Cricket and socialiser. I was not studious and struggled to pass examinations albeit that might have been because I spent my final year romancing the local girl's school hockey captain. I was impressed that she passed all her examinations and went on to the prestigious sporting centre of Loughborough College. She was Scottish and her mother did not like me.

Having failed to get to university I took the easy way out by persuading my father to arrange for me to start working for the Midland Bank. I made one condition which seemed to please my mother and insisted on leaving home so ending up in the carpet town of Kidderminster. This part of Worcestershire is particularly picturesque and three miles to the west is the Georgian town of Bewdley nestling on the banks of the Severn. This rises in the Cambrian mountains in Mid Wales and, at 220 miles, is the longest river in Great Britain. It was not too long before I managed to persuade Judy, the manager's secretary, to walk along the tow path with me when I was not playing rugby for Kidderminster.

A starting salary enabled me to purchase my first motor car: a light blue Austin Mini now considered to be an icon of 1960s British popular culture. The innovative transverse engine and front-wheel layout was designed for the British Motor Corporation by Sir Alec Issigonis and my vehicle was made at the Longbridge factory just south of Northfield in Birmingham where I was born. I cleaned it every other day.

Although I liked Kidderminster, I was restless and yearned to be back in Birmingham. The terms for my future direction of travel were set by Judy and I announcing our engagement. We are still married fifty-four years after our wedding. I nervously confronted the manager and, to my great relief, the bank moved me back to Birmingham where we bought our first house: an end-of-terrace property on the Bournville Estate for which we paid £3,650. In the early morning one could smell the chocolate wafting over from the Cadbury factories.

The earlier mention of 'Dad's Army' connects to an event involving a future celebrity. One Saturday afternoon we were driving back from Kidderminster, where Judy's parents lived, to our new home when we decided to stop at a favourite pub, The Bell at Belbroughton on the edge of the Clee Hills. At one point I visited the facilities, returning to find that a good-looking man was chatting up my new wife. There was no need to challenge him because he was someone I recognised. Our parents had attended the Northfield Methodist Church, on the south side of Birmingham, and their son and I knew each other from Sunday School and later playing rugby in opposition when our schools met in competition. It was Ian Lavender, who was finishing his stage training at the Bristol Vic Old Theatre School and who, shortly afterwards, landed the role of Private Pike in 'Dad's Army'. The comedy show, based on Britain's wartime Home Guard, was first televised on 31 July 1968 and ran for eighty episodes, a film and stage show. Fifty years later the programmes are still being repeated on various television channels. Ian was most certainly not guilty of being what Captain Mainwaring suggested that he (as Private Pike) was – a 'stupid boy'! Now aged seventy-seven, he is the last surviving member of the original main cast.

We're all shooting for the stars

By the spring of 1969, Judy and I were happily settled into our new home (despite the early morning smell of chocolate) and our respective jobs. Life was good. The Labour prime minister, Harold Wilson, was coming to the end of his tenure and, in the June 1970 general election, lost power to the Conservative leader Edward Heath. He immediately began a formal entry application for the United Kingdom to join the European Communities ('EC'), better known as the Common Market, which was ratified on 1 January 1973.

The 1969 FA Cup was won 1 – 0 by Manchester City (defeating Leicester City) and David Bowie had a huge hit with 'Space Oddity'. He was not the only one with a planetary vision. On 20 July 1969 the American Moon Commander Neil Armstrong became the first man to walk on the lunar surface followed by Lunar Module Pilot, Buzz Aldrin, while the third member of the crew, Pilot Michael Collins, controlled the space capsule.

My attention was focused on more earthly events and in particular playing rugby. Physicality, the aggressive domination of one person over another, is a recurring theme in sporting life.

In the boxing ring American heavyweight Mike Tyson, known as 'Iron Mike' and 'the baddest man on the planet', now 56, is considered by many to be the most ferocious boxer of all time. In 1997, he was disqualified in a championship title match for biting off part of Evander Holyfield's right ear.

On the football pitch Vinnie Jones, now 57, was part of the Wimbledon side known as the 'Crazy Gang' and transferred his hard-earned image for, at times, excessive aggression to the cinema screen, playing a series of roles as a violent criminal.

In rugby union, many consider the South African second row forward Bakkies Botha as the most violent player of all time. He was known as 'the Enforcer'. He was suspended a number of times for a range of offences including head-butting, kicking and punching. He was a member of the Springboks side which triumphed in the World Cup in 2007 and won numerous titles and awards. Now 43, he runs a business in South Africa called 'Bakkies the Butcher'.

Before and after returning from Kidderminster to Birmingham, I played in the back row of the rugby scrum for King Edwards Five Ways Old Edwardians from 1964 – 1970 when I broke my shoulder after suffering a late tackle against Nuneaton. My employer, Midland Bank Limited, was not happy about the amount of time I was away and so I took up the game of squash racquets.

Nigel Horton: the hardest rugby player I ever met

Two years earlier I had been selected for the Midlands Colts who I captained for a season. Rugby Union was not the game that is played now. There were fifteen players each side and a referee plus two linesmen who did no more than hold their flag in the air when the ball went out of play. Compare that with the modern game: substitutes, red and yellow cards, the modern technology used with better referees and endless television replays to ensure decisions are made correctly.

It was the law of the jungle on the rugby pitch and I came across a player who is perhaps the most physical character I ever experienced. Nigel Horton was born in Birmingham and was a police cadet. He was selected in the second row in all the matches the Midland Colts played. He was massive and formed part of a formidable pack of eight forwards: he was the leader from the front.

On a drizzly, miserable Saturday afternoon in Leicester in front of a partisan crowd we found ourselves playing Leicestershire Colts and it was attrition from the start. For the first time the pack was going backwards and I was working overtime trying to create a unity of purpose. Our scrum half was having a torrid time as their forwards poured through the lineout. I could see that Nigel was being diverted from his usual game by an opposite number who was as tall as him albeit he was amazingly thin and wiry. I spotted that he was talking to Nigel which I thought was a little misguided.

There was a break in play for an injured player to be treated and, as we formed the next lineout, a selector on the touchline grabbed my arm and hissed, "Nigel's having problems. Start a fight." I called the ball long and as it reached my opposite number, I hit him. War broke out as my opponent took exception to my actions and belted me to high heaven. As I was collapsing to the ground, I caught sight out of my closing eye of Nigel's opposite number going up into the afternoon sky like a wobbly beanpole. Nigel had hit him under the chin when everyone's attention was elsewhere. As we ran to the next scrum he grunted "Thanks." We dominated the battles and won the war.

Nigel played for Moseley from 1969 – 1980 and for England twenty times. He then became one of the first English players to move to France and joined Toulouse where he settled into the ferocity of some of the most violent club rugby ever played. He was known as 'Le Demon Blanc', the white devil.

During the last match I played with him against the Welsh Colts in a mudbath near Bridgend, one of their forwards took a kick at Nigel and lacerated his leg. He was in agony. The hard men of my side gathered around him and demanded to know which Welshman had inflicted the damage. Nigel looked up and said, "I give it, I take it."

*****

A year after my rugby career faltered so did my time with Midland Bank and as a result my father stopped speaking to me. He simply could not comprehend what I had done. He had spent five years from 1939 to 1945 fighting the Germans with General Montgomery across North Africa, up the west coast of Italy and back through Europe. He was pleased, if not a little surprised (as I was), that I managed to scrape through the banking examinations and qualify as a Member of the Institute of Bankers; the royal assent, and thus the title 'Chartered Institute', came in 1987. He was perplexed when he learned that, in his words, I had committed professional hara-kiri. Those were his thoughts. I saw it differently. I resigned from the Midland Bank and joined a secondary bank.

It was not until the end of the nineteen seventies that there was a statutory definition of a bank. Most people, if asked, would have defined the term by saying 'Barclays, Lloyds or Midland' bank. However, from the late nineteen sixties there emerged an aggressive group of finance houses which became known as 'secondary banks'. The Edward Heath Conservative government was focused on the 'Barber Boom' – named after the Chancellor of the Exchequer Anthony Barber – and the introduction in 1971 of 'Competition and Credit Control'. The effect was to release vast amounts of new money into the system. A group of finance houses climbed aboard and, crucially, had access to the money markets. They borrowed short and lent long which is the surest way of creating a financial problem termed 'illiquidity'.

Amongst the finance houses to take advantage of this opportunity was Mercantile Credit, one of the largest of the hire purchase companies. They formed their own 'secondary bank': Astley Acceptances Limited. One day I read a job advertisement in the local paper seeking the recruitment of a banking assistant. I applied, went to Manchester for an interview, was offered the position, resigned from the Midland Bank and told my father.

The Astley Acceptances team in Birmingham specialised in lending on businesses and became a leading name in the business transfer market. This involved financing purchasers of both freehold and leasehold concerns such as newsagents/confectionary/tobacconists, sub-post offices, public houses and restaurants. I was in my element generating new business from business transfer agents (estate agents who specialised in selling businesses), interviewing prospective clients, vetting the businesses and visiting the Mercantile Credit training school at Stoke Poges in Buckinghamshire to explain what we did. This gave me exposure to the Mercantile Credit directors.

Judy and Tony Drury were booming as encouraged by the Government. We moved out to Droitwich in Worcestershire and I recall queuing for three hours to put fifty pounds down on a plot of ground for our new house. Judy worked for a firm of lawyers and drove a blue Triumph Spitfire; we travelled around playing a CD featuring a former Beatle who had started a solo career. From his 1971 album of the same name, John Lennon asked us to 'imagine' a world of peace without materialism. We were happy to sing along although we resisted the suggestion. This was because I had spotted a bigger house and we bought it. I wrote to my general manager in London asking to increase my mortgage which elicited a phone call from him.

"Ah, Drury. Yes. Right. No." I was deflated but held my nerve.

"I do hope, sir, that your decision doesn't reflect any dissatisfaction with my performance here?" I pleaded or rather grovelled.

"Er, what? No," he stuttered. "It's a little complicated. Confidential, rather. I want to meet you as soon as possible. I'll drive out from London and you come down the M1 to junction 11 and we'll have a coffee together. Tomorrow. Bye."

Twenty-four hours later I found myself in the restaurant at Whipsnade Zoo drinking coffee with my general manager. We had met at junction 11, he told me to follow him, up the A5 we went and took the turning for the zoo. Crazy.

"You've been chosen," he said.

And I had. The chairman of Mercantile Credit, A Victor Adey, was leading a massive re-organisation of the Group into three divisions: consumer credit, leasing and banking. I was to head up the London Banking Office. Even Judy was impressed although her mother expressed doubts because London was so far from Wales.

The pace did not slow. We put our house up for sale at a price of £13,500, decided that the Euston train line into the capital offered optimum commuter travel, and bought a house in an area of beautiful trees, Redwood Glade, in the market town of Leighton Buzzard mainly because it was adjacent to a wonderful squash club which was to play a significant part in my future life.

I settled quickly into London life based in offices near

to Holborn Tube Station and built a relationship with Roy Simblett from Nottingham who headed the London leasing division and Paul Blake from Wales, the accountant. He was less introspective than myself and, together with Roy, we adopted a pub in High Holborn called 'The Bunghole' with its rickety chairs and sawdust-covered floors where we met most days for a working lunch.

Paul would take us through the latest news on the miners' strike leading to the Conservative Prime Minister Edward Heath's declaring of a state of emergency. Another problem he faced was the ongoing controversy following 'Bloody Sunday' in early 1972 in Northern Ireland when British soldiers opened fire on unarmed civilians during a protest march in the Bogside area of Derry and, later, the burning down of the British embassy in Dublin. Roy regaled us with his interest in American politics, albeit US President Richard Nixon's Watergate difficulties were on the front pages of the national press. Roy proved to be the 'boffin' who would later know that the Americans dropped over six million tons of bombs on North Vietnam and lost the war. My contribution was to offer a review of Andrew Lloyd Webber's controversial stage show 'Jesus Christ Superstar' which was playing at the Palace Theatre in Covent Garden which I was to see three times.

My main preoccupation was to settle Judy down in Leighton Buzzard which proved to be the easier of my tasks and to maximise the opportunity given to me by Mercantile Credit. My father was now speaking to me. The chairman invited Paul, Roy and myself into lunch and grilled us one by one. It was explosive. I had made it. I was on the way up, but not quite as I was expecting. Not for the first time in my life, the damage was done by a London political leader.

*****

(John) Jeremy Thorpe (29 April 1929 – 4 December 2014) was Member of Parliament for North Devon from 1959 to

1979 and leader of the Liberal Party from 1967 to 1976. In May 1979 he was tried at the Old Bailey on charges of conspiracy and incitement to murder his boyfriend, Norman Scott, a former model. Although acquitted of all charges, his political career was in tatters. In the mid-eighties he became disabled by Parkinson's disease. In his later years he became a supporter of human rights and an opponent of apartheid.

The Secondary Banking Crash 1973 –1975

It would be misleading to suggest that Jeremy Thorpe caused the event which was to shatter my career. I settled down enthusiastically into the Mercantile Credit reorganisation and began to recruit staff and develop the London Banking Division. I imagine I was aware of the underlying political tensions as events developed including rising interest rates, an oil crisis as the Organisation of Petroleum Producing Counties (OPEC) increased their prices by 300% and the start of a property collapse. I was becoming concerned that our house in Droitwich was not selling despite having reduced the asking price by £1,000. The staff director was unhelpful. "Drury," he sermonised, "you simply aren't going to make the profit you were expecting to achieve." I tried to argue that I had bought a house in Leighton Buzzard on the basis of selling our Worcestershire home for £13,500 but he was not at home.

Despite these warning signs, the crash when it came in November 1973 was a complete surprise and Jeremy Thorpe was not blameless. He was a director of London and Counties Securities which became mired in controversy. It collapsed as the money markets refused to renew its short-term debts and this precipitated a wholesale withdrawal by lenders from the secondary banking sector and, in all, around thirty companies became distressed. The Bank of England gathered together the leaders of the main banks and together they created a 'lifeboat fund' to provide liquidity for these companies including Mercantile Credit.

One of the best books written about these events was 'The Secondary Banking Crisis, 1973-75: its causes and course' (MacMillan 1982). The author was a financial journalist, Margaret Reid, who was well respected in the Square Mile. She contacted me during her research having read some of my articles in 'Bankers' Magazine' (explained in Chapter Two) which were to become a key factor in my future career. We had lunch together at an Italian restaurant and, apart from her Edwardian style, it was her fascinating insight into the workings of the City which made it a rewarding occasion. I recall that towards the end of lunch the waiter approached our table and asked my guest if she would like to see the cheese board. Margaret waved her arm and then watched as the three-tier server was wheeled towards us: there must have been perhaps twelve varieties including Cheddar, Camembert, Roquefort and Wensleydale. She asked to sample each of them. She then looked at the waiter and said, "No, thank you."

My general manager called me in to his office and told me to stop all lending because there was no money. I was to get back what I could from the loans we had made and when I suggested that would not keep me busy, he suggested I went to the library – which was an improvement on Whipsnade Zoo. Then the rumours began to circulate as it became known that the chairman was on the warpath and heads would roll. My general manager contacted me early one morning and told me to be prepared for an event after lunch.

The afternoon arrived slowly because the whole of the senior management knew that at three o'clock we were to be told our fate. There were around eighteen of us summoned to the Mercantile Credit boardroom facing the chairman and the board of directors. A Victor Adey began by lecturing us on the collapse of the financial markets and emphasising how hard he had been working to re-build the company. This was before he would be boarding his chauffeur-driven Rolls Royce and returning home to his country mansion. "I have been able to retain some of you," he announced. All the directors stayed in place and my increasingly cynical self-wondered if they awarded themselves pay rises for 'saving' the company?

Then the slow death began. A Victor Adey stared around the room, picked up his list, and pointed his finger at the first person in the circle of defendants. To my horror I realised I was second last if he followed his intended trajectory. My pal, the leasing man Roy Simblett was third in line. The first, a debt-collections manager called Collins, faced the punitive digit. "Collins," announced the chairman, "you're going." Jerry, with whom I played squash, stood up and walked out of the room. He told me later he already had another job lined up and just wanted the pay-off.

Victor Adey moved on to someone I did not know and then to Roy who remained impassive. "Simblett," he announced, "you're staying." I wondered what the message was to be for me. The next victim was a rather effeminate computer manager who was told, "You're going" whereupon he burst into tears and rushed from the room. The directors remained impassive, probably planning their evening at the opera or, in several cases, dinner with one of the tenth-floor secretaries.

A Victor Adey seemed to be tiring of this version of the Nuremberg Trials and speeded up. My accountant associate Paul Blake survived – not that it did him too much good because, a heavy smoker, he died of lung cancer at a young age. As I watched the chairman continue the agony, I felt his finger resembled an Assegai spear used so brutally by the Xhosa tribe of the Cape Province of South Africa. Three to go before my fate was announced.

My life seemed to be swimming in front of my eyes: a beautiful young wife, a fearsome Welsh mother-in-law, a house mortgage I could not afford, a car where the monthly payments were double my spare cash, a house in Droitwich that would not sell and a professional qualification which was for a sector now in disarray.

"Drury," boomed the chairman.

I now know how Marie Antoinette felt around twelve-fifteen in Paris on 16 October 1793 at the Place de la Revolution (now the Place de la Concorde) as the blade of the guillotine hurtled downwards towards her frail neck. It is recorded that she had said to her executioner, having stepped on his foot, "Pardon me, sir, I did not do it on purpose."

I decided to follow a similar pathway to finality.

"Pardon me, Chairman, I did not come to London to have my head chopped off. YOU brought me down here."

"Drury, you're staying."

*****

I stopped drinking alcohol at the age of sixty. I don't think we made good bedfellows. I wish I had resisted at an earlier age. Firoza, my secretary who worked with me in the nineteen eighties, once said to me, "I wish you wouldn't have the third glass of wine."

A group of Mercantile Credit survivors went to the pub on the corner of Great Queen Street and set about consuming pint after pint. I suppose we were selfish, in one way, with so many of our pals jobless and facing hardship. Now I know how I would feel if I was ejected from 'Love Island'. I can't recall reaching Euston Station or which train I boarded. The next thing I knew was being shaken by a train guard. As I looked out into the dark of the station platform, I informed him rather forcefully that this was not Leighton Buzzard. "Correct," he said, "you're in Northampton."

Staggering out to the taxi rank where a rather stroppy driver took out his chart and advised me of the cost of being transported back thirty miles to my Redwood Glade home, I exclaimed, "How much?" and added, "I'll have to re-mortgage my house." This was a silly thing to say because my mortgage was with Mercantile Credit and they had made it clear there were no more increases available.

I slumped into the back seat but the driver had not finished with me.

"If you throw up in my taxi, I'll double the fare," he growled.

The evening could not get any worse. Judy greeted me at the front door. "Tony, wonderful news. My mother is coming to stay with us."

****

CHAPTER TWO
THE PHONEY WAR, TRAINING DUTIES AND THE START OF THE REAL WAR

After Nazi Germany invaded Poland in September 1939 until eight months later in May 1940, when the invasion of France commenced, there was virtually no military action in Western Europe. An American Senator is credited with saying that the period of inactivity suggested to him, "there is something phoney about this war." Thus, the term 'phoney war' entered military terminology.

A similar atmosphere transcended Mercantile Credit after the rescue by the Bank of England, the 'big' banks and their 'lifeboat fund': nothing happened. The initial relief that we were still employed was overtaken by frustration and impatience in the face of an information blackout. My general manager clearly was not in the loop and seemed to spend most of his time moving files around his desk.

The political situation was unstable and Conservative Prime Minister Edward Heath, in February 1974, called a general election using the slogan 'Who Governs Britain?' and, facing a need to enter coalition with the Liberals, failed and resigned. Labour leader Harold Wilson became a minority prime minister albeit he secured a marginal overall victory in a further general election in October of the same year. But for him there was danger lurking in the shape of a steel-reinforced passionate opponent.

The speaker in the chiffon dress has much to say

She was stung when the television critic Clive James compared her voice to "a cat sliding down a blackboard". The future prime minister was to work hard at improving her presentational skills. But in 1976, three years before she won a momentous general election, Margaret Thatcher addressed a gathering of her supporters at a dinner held in her parliamentary seat of Finchley, north London. Already her controversial views were making waves but it was her foreign policy speech given that evening, titled in advance, 'Britain awake', that created a political reaction. She said, "I stand before you in my Red Star chiffon evening gown, my face softly made up and my fair hair gently waved, the Iron Lady of the western world." A Soviet journalist picked this up and, in a reference to her ruthless and uncompromising style, labelled her the 'Iron Lady'.

It was a signpost to the future of British politics. Her rise to power continued unabated and, following the Conservative's general election victory in May 1979, she was to touch everyone's life, not always to their approval. In my case her approach to enterprise was to have a significant impact on my progress although I was, at this point in my career, struggling to see a future for myself and my family.

Whilst following politics, my mind was on our financial position and applying myself to improving my game of squash helped by the fact that next to Redwood Glade, where our expensive house was located, was the Knolls Squash Club. A local businessman had bought the Grade II listed building and added six squash courts partly because his son was ranked in the top ten UK players. The growing popularity of the sport was particularly down to a Cornish-born Irishman. Jonah Barrington (now 81) discovered the game and dedicated himself to winning a contest he described as 'boxing with racquets' by being the fittest player ever. He gained publicity by taking part in Television's 'Superstars' in 1975/76 which included events such as weightlifting, gymnastics, cycling and a 600 metres steeplechase. He won the British Open championship (effectively the world title) six times between 1967 – 1973. He was perhaps a little outspoken on various topics but his personal application to fitness and winning was inspirational.

24

Barrington was right. The game of squash played in an enclosed space (glass walls came later) was pugilistic and at times dangerous. I was never a talented exponent but I was fit and determined and qualified as a squash coach and referee. The only time I was actually hurt was, when on holiday in Portugal, I agreed to train some holidaymakers at a local club. As we finished a session, I asked the group if they had enjoyed themselves whereupon a teenager lashed out and hit the ball into my eye. Ouch. The squash ball is like a rubbery plum and gains heat as a game is played. When Barrington won the British Open title in 1968 his opponent, the Egyptian player Abou Taleb, hit him with the ball six times on the lower leg and thigh but still lost the match. I met Jonah several times and always enjoyed his verbose company.

The gladiatorial exertions of the squash court did not compensate for the phoney war taking place at Mercantile Credit and so I followed the advice of my general manager and went to the library in Holborn. My attention was drawn to the sports section where I discovered a book which came to have an influence on my future life.

'Be Fit! Or Be Damned!' By Percy Cerutty

The opening paragraphs set the tone from the beginning:

Any book on health and fitness must start with what man is – his physical body, the nature of his mind and the needs of both!

The high incidence of death from diseases of the circulatory system…as well as the lethal strokes due to artery lesion in the brain…together with Carcinoma (cancer in its many forms) account for perhaps 90 per cent of all deaths.

Yet these diseases are preventable.

It was written in 1967 and the misogynistic style reflected

more the times than any lack of gender respect on Cerutty's part. He was an eccentric Australian athletics coach who pioneered a system of 'Stotan' training which embraced a holistic regime of natural diets, hard training in coastal surroundings and mental stimulation. The term was created by Cerutty and is a combination of the two words 'stoic' and 'spartan'.

He founded a training camp on the seashore at Portsea near to Melbourne in the State of Victoria where he coached Australian Herb Elliot to a series of world record performances culminating in his Olympic gold medal in the 1,500 metres at the 1960 Rome Games. He was appointed a Member of the British Empire (MBE) in 1972 for his services to sport and physical fitness. He died from motor neurone disease in 1975 at the age of 80.

It is the simplistic style of writing which adds to one's reaction to the twenty-one chapters each dissecting an aspect of human physiology: food, longevity, the heart, lungs, liver and kidneys, the brain, emotions, blood pressure, stress and ulcers, de-naturalised foods (the destroyers) on and on. The underlying theme was that by maximising personal fitness and your physiological regime the body would fulfil its potential and, when the time came, would simply cease working, painlessly.

I never came anywhere near to achieving what Cerutty advocated due to an unhealthy appetite and a propensity to socialise a little too much but I have retained a copy of his book (which is regularly re-published) on my desk and occasionally re-read a passage or two. In a later chapter I will explain how I came to create a charity dedicated to helping people achieve a healthy lifestyle by controlling and, if needed, by losing weight. I wish I could have met the great man.

But I was fit and determined, bored to death at work and financially hard up. It took us two years to sell our house in Droitwich for £11,500 – well short of the original asking price – and so we had little spare cash. Then the call came, out of the blue, and I was on my way to a 'big' bank training school. Even my father was impressed.

'Appletons': guess who is coming to dinner?

The news broke that Mercantile Credit was being acquired by Barclays Bank and I found myself being delegated to attend the Barclays Bank Training Centre situated in Ashdown Forest in southern England, just off the M23 motorway, to explain what we did. As far as the bank managers attending the courses were concerned, I was a hire-purchase salesman: the banter was hurtful but fun. Almost imperceptibly the atmosphere started to improve and I found myself being booked to give talks every two weeks and then I was invited to stay for the evening and attend their dinners with accommodation provided. However, nothing prepared me for the next event in my career.

I received a summons from Mercantile Credit head office to attend a meeting with the new chairman, Stuart Errington, a rather different personality from A Victor Adey who had retired. He did not mess around. I was being moved to become training manager at the Mercantile Credit centre at Stoke Poges in Buckinghamshire. I was there for three years from 1975 to 1977 and relished every moment.

The early skirmishes were interesting. Every two weeks a course was held for Mercantile Credit branch managers at 'Appletons', a country house in two acres of Buckinghamshire parkland, which was run by a couple (Harry and Peggy who looked after the property and prepared buffet lunches. The classroom accommodated sixteen attendees and the teaching was delivered by a combination of outside professional trainers, visitors from head office and the training manager (guess who?). I quickly picked up one trick. Head office directors and senior management looked upon a call to 'Appletons' to participate in a particular session as rather special and my popularity soared. I also learned the hard way that the afternoon session after lunch was known in academic circles as 'the graveyard' as students slept off their lunches. If a director pushed me too much, I awarded him a graveyard spot.

"Er, Drury, did you feel I went down well today?" they would plead.

"You were scintillating, sir," I would reply and then quietly chuckle to myself.

The managers were accommodated in local hotels and every other Sunday afternoon I would drive down to Heathrow Airport to meet the Scottish and Irish managers flying in. I enjoyed waiting in the busy transport hub witnessing some amazing incidences as global travellers lost their luggage, missed their connections or simply fell out with each other. On the first occasion there were two Scottish managers to meet. The training co-ordinator had written down for me 'Iain McDonald and Hamish Scott, Flight SCO80. ETA 17.00.' The twenty-four-hour clock was too much for me as I arrived just before seven o'clock. McDonald was quite reasonable about my late appearance and was comfortably settled at the airport bar. Scott saw things differently.

"I dinna know much about ye Drury but I'm no impressed," he informed me.

The highlight of each week was the training course dinner held at a local hotel and nearly always attended by the chairman and several senior directors. Stuart Errington had a powerful personality and placed an importance on the training school which he determined should reflect the corporate culture. He always allowed a 'questions and answers' session towards the end of each dinner and his honesty and clarity of thought were impressive.

We all make mistakes and I managed to achieve a humdinger. In the alternative weeks when there was not a training course, I would visit the regions, meet with the senior management and discuss the work of 'Appletons'. I noticed that in almost every Mercantile Credit branch there would be a senior representative and an office manager who was nearly always a female colleague. I submitted a proposal to my boss suggesting we included these two categories in the training schedule. Almost immediately the representatives started to attend courses and were a success. They were out there every day in the marketplace negotiating with car dealers and other third-party introducers of transactions thus generating new business; their experiences at the sharp end were invaluable to the training process. Well done, Tony Drury.

The suggestion that senior girls (the term used by Mercantile Credit) should attend courses caused confusion and division and eventually was decided at a board meeting of the directors. One opinionated director called me into his office and glared.

"Do you realise, Drury," he almost shouted, "that firstly no husband is going to allow his wife to attend a course at 'Appletons', that hire-purchase is a man's world and you are proposing that they stay in the same hotel as the men. Are you mad?!"

The board of directors approved the scheme mainly because Stuart Errington supported the idea and wanted it to happen. A notice was issued to all the regions and my coordinator received a number of applications from 'senior girls' across the United Kingdom. The first 'mixed' course was prepared and on Sunday afternoon I travelled to Heathrow Airport to meet two attendees from Scotland and Northern Ireland. I made certain I was on time at 5.00pm (17.00 hours). The office manager from Dundee, who was called Elspeth, was a little nervous; the senior representative from Belfast, called Michael (not Mike, he insisted), was charming. On Monday morning the course programme started well and the six 'girls' who were attending dazzled all of us with their knowledge and commitment.

Thursday evening neared and I prepared the class for the dinner ahead. My boss took me to one side. He was concerned that Stuart Errington and the head office directors, most of whom had booked hotel rooms, should not see any 'hanky-panky' (his word) between the representatives and the 'girls'. I assured my boss that I had gained an impression that the ladies were well able to look after themselves.

The course dinner was a great success. Stuart Errington was regal and continually changed places so that he sat, at any one time, by each of the six 'girls'. They were splendid in their evening outfits and were being careful with their drinks. I met my boss, who was worrying about any nocturnal activity, early on Friday morning. I told him all seemed settled except that I could not account for two of the 'girls' whose bedrooms, according to the hotel receptionist, had not been occupied the previous evening. He became agitated and reminded me that I had guaranteed that there would be no problems in that direction. I accepted his reprimand and then told him that I could not account for two of the directors.

'The pen is mightier than the sword.'

So wrote the playwright Edward Bulwer-Lytton in his 1839 historical play about Cardinal Richelieu. The chief minister to King Louis XIII was unable to take up arms against his plotters and suggested that the written word could defeat aggression.

My growing status at 'Appletons' regenerated my ambition and I wanted to maximise the opportunity given to me. The one priceless advantage I had was that I was acquiring financial knowledge rather quickly. I listened to every lecture delivered by the professional trainers and from the managers, representatives and office staff. I was becoming proficient in instalment credit law including the Hire Purchase Acts of 1938, 1954 and 1964/65 and then along came The Consumer Credit Act 1974 which established a licensing system covering all those engaged in consumer credit and consumer hire and extended consumer protection through the provisions of Section 75. This increased liability to Mercantile Credit where, under unsecured personal loans and hire-purchase agreements, it assumed the same responsibilities as the actual supplier of the goods, up to a maximum of £10,000. Section 75 has been amended many times since and is an important responsibility for credit card companies.

I knew Eric Glover, the Secretary-General of the Institute of Bankers. Eric liked his City lunches and soon we began to meet regularly and a suggestion was made that I start writing for their Journal. Before long I was contributing every other month and extended the subjects covered to include the leasing of vehicles and plant and machinery. I did not know too much about this new facility, leasing, which offered tax advantages especially for higher value transactions but crucially understood a little more than most other people, which made me an expert. This is rather like the current cryptocurrency (from bitcoin to blockchain) sector at the moment where most people have little idea what it is but are climbing on the bandwagon in the hopes of making personal fortunes and thereby creating a haven for the fraudsters.

At the 1979 Mercantile Credit planning conference held in Maidenhead the first morning session began with a rather self-important director of the group's leasing arm showing a blank slide on the screen. "That," he said to a room full of hire-purchase salesmen, "is the amount of new business you lot will transact today." That generated a ripple of uncertain laughter. The director then put up a second slide which showed '£10 million' in large characters and bright colours. "That," he announced, "is the value of the amount of leasing business transacted by our London office this morning." His statement killed off the planning conference for the rest of the day until the hotel bar opened.

In 1995 at Southwark Crown Court, Leonard Bartlett, out on a record £10 million bail, was found guilty of a complex computer leasing fraud which lost banks and finance houses around £23 million. He was sentenced to five years in prison.

I was contacted by the editor of 'Bankers' Magazine', a monthly publication from the BPCC stable of titles, who commissioned me to write a series of articles on instalment credit and leasing. I started to receive letters from readers and several telephone calls but then came a rather important message: Stuart Errington wanted to see me.

I sat in his office, respectful but a little apprehensive. More than anything I was hoping that my time at training school would result in a promotion (and an increase in salary) and I would be returning to one of the new business divisions. The outcome was two out of three. The chairman was fulsome in his praise for my work at 'Appletons' and I was being promoted to assistant general manager (I mentally calculated which debts I could start paying off). He then dropped his bombshell. I was being moved to Head of Corporate Planning. I suspect he sensed my disappointment but he assured me it would be a stepping stone in my career.

In 1977 I moved into a cramped office in Great Queen Street (just off Covent Garden) and started work as a corporate planner. I disliked it from the start. My predecessor, an Eton-educated nephew of one of the directors, thought that the whole thing was a 'wizz'. He was seriously bright and wrote the annual Mercantile Credit plan in around six weeks and spent much of the rest of the year testing the wines to be served at the planning conference dinners. He disappeared and I sat at my desk, head in hands.

I and my small team organised the annual planning conference held at a Maidenhead hotel for three years. I tried hard to make sense of the process but actually hated every moment. At the 1978 conference, on the first evening, the North-Eastern regional director came up to me with a bag of personal washing and told me to get it cleaned for him.

The variable working hours enabled me to attend to several pressing domestic matters. Christopher Paul Drury arrived in May 1977 and Emma Suzanne Drury in August 1978 and I had serious responsibilities to fulfil.

For the first time at Mercantile Credit, I asked to be moved and was 'rewarded' by a transfer, in 1981, to an administration division. The chairman said it would be good for my career. I discovered that I was controlling a total of over one hundred people who were involved in various activities including instalment credit payments and outstanding collections, the issuing of customer statements and other processes. One day I was told that a particular member of staff was causing difficulties and had been absent for three days. I invited her into my office. She lived in Willesden in a one-bedroomed flat and had been unable to leave it for two days because of street unrest. On the third morning she was trying to find care for her baby daughter. Welcome to the real world, Drury.

Out of the blue I received an approach from the managing director of 'Bankers' Magazine'. Waterlow Publishers wanted me to write a book on finance houses.

'Finance Houses: Their Development and Role in the Modern Financial Sector'

My book was published in 1982 and one year later I was made a Fellow of the Institute of Bankers for my contribution to the bibliography of the industry. I recall standing outside Elizabethan House in Great Queen Street, the head office of Mercantile Credit, looking up at the tenth floor where the directors resided, wondering what I should do. I took out an invitation I had received and decided to go along. It was a drinks party to celebrate the signing of an agreement to merge 'The Institute of Banker's Journal' with 'Bankers' Magazine' into a new publication. Eric Glover had mentioned it to me but my frustrations at Mercantile Credit were dominating my thinking.

I went along to the Dorchester Hotel in Park Lane, Westminster, and immediately realised that this was a lavish occasion. The ballroom was heaving with bankers, politicians, lords of the Realm, judges and glamorous hostesses. I immediately met a number of people I knew including a slightly inebriated Eric Glover.

"You must meet Captain Bob," he slurred and then disappeared.

My brain began to work overtime. Robert Maxwell, a man never out of the headlines including his ongoing battles with Rupert Murdoch. I moved to the edge of the room and found a press release. It explained the brilliant deal agreed by the publisher of 'Bankers' Magazine', R. Maxwell, with 'The Institute of Banker's Journal' to merge the two into a new publication, 'Banking World'.

I looked across the ballroom and there standing aloof was a tall, huge, dark-haired man. I found a waiter and quickly drank a glass of wine before approaching the host for the evening. He looked at me and I pounced.

"Mr Maxwell," I said, "you don't know who I am but you published my book and I wanted to thank you."

His voice was uniquely sonorous, deep, measured and powerful. He looked at me.

"Mr Drury. I do know who you are. You will come and see me."

When I looked up, he had moved on. Although I was yet to realise the consequences, I had stuck my head above the parapet.

*****

"You will come and see me" resonated around my head as I travelled back home. I wondered if this might be a significant moment in my career. Then I wondered what I had to do to respond to his invitation. I was to discover that Robert Maxwell was an insomniac who had three secretaries, two based at Maxwell House in Worship Street in central London and one at Headington Hall in Oxford, reputedly the largest council house ever known. It was here that he lived with his family and where several companies were based.

The next day I used my lunchtime to slip along to Maxwell House and managed to gain access to one of his secretaries who made an appointment for me to meet the Chairman of the British Printing & Communication Company (BPCC) the following Tuesday at 6.00pm. I spent the weekend researching everything I could find about the history and success of Robert Maxwell.

I arrived at Maxwell House in Worship Street, adjacent to Finsbury Square, comfortably before the allocated time, reported to the secretary and was told to sit in the waiting room where I watched people come and go. There was an intensity about people's body language and I was perplexed by the number of employees who appeared to be on various errands.

There are numerous stories about 'Captain Bob', as the press labelled him, because, as I was to discover, he was restless and animated. The waiting room is where one famous event took place. A male in his twenties was seated and smoking. Maxwell abhorred the practice and, on seeing an employee puffing away, stormed up to him and demanded to know how much a month he earned. On hearing the amount stated he took out his wallet and thrust the money into the hands of the startled man. "You're fired," boomed the Chairman. "Get out." The visiting salesman from a catering company left the building clutching his unexpected bonus.

6.15pm came and went and I checked in again with the secretary who waved me away. It was not until 7.30pm that I was shown into the Chairman's palatial office. It was huge, Maxwell was huge, his desk was huge and he was on the telephone speaking in what I decided was an Eastern European language. He indicated that I should sit down. I did so and to my relief there was no unexpected sound.

From 1976 to 1979, the BBC ran a comedy series, 'The Fall

and Rise of Reginal Perrin.' It starred Leonard Rossiter whose job at Sunshine Desserts led to some bizarre behaviour. Occasionally he had to meet with his overbearing boss, CJ (played by John Barron) who had a desk that was higher that the visitor's seat. When Reginald Perrin sat down on the visitor's chair it emitted a loud squeaking sound. Rossiter was known for his series of advertisements set on an airplane where he poured Cinzano over Joan Collins. He was a keen squash player. He died aged 57.

"Mr Drury," said Robert Maxwell. "Why have you come to see me?"

The wrong answer was 'because you told me to.'

The right answer was, "Chairman, you have created a brilliant initiative with your merger of 'The Institute of Banker's Journal' and 'Bankers' Magazine' and 'Banking World' will become a lasting testimony to your creativity. I would like to be the editor, please."

For the only time in our future relationship, the Chairman hesitated.

"Er … you can't be the editor. Peter Jay (more later) is appointing one. I want you to be the managing director of Waterlow Publishers. Do you want to think about it?"

I stood up. I have no idea why.

"Chairman," I replied. "I've thought about the position. It will be a privilege to work under your leadership."

Maxwell stood up and indicated that I should follow him. We strode down a corridor so, as I was to learn, we could meet the chairman of Waterlow Publishers.

Sam Silkin, The Lord Silkin of Dulwich, PC, QC (now KC) was the Labour member of parliament for Dulwich from 1964 to 1983. He was the Attorney General for England, Wales and Northern Ireland from 1974 to 1979. He died at the age of 70.

Maxwell burst into his office and told Sam that he wanted to introduce the new managing director of

Waterlow Publishers. Silkin stood up and, as was to manifest in the weeks ahead (although we became strong working colleagues), spluttered and gasped before informing Maxwell that there was an MD of Waterlow Publishers – whereupon he was told to sort it out.

*****

The contract of employment came in the next three days and a starting date agreed. Maxwell doubled my salary and gave me a car. Judy, Chris, Emma and Tony Drury were on their way back up the greasy pole of working in the Square Mile.

Maxwell's signature on the covering letter and my contract, and, as I was to discover, his handwriting, was an illegible scrawl. There was a reason for this. Jan Hoch was born on 10 June 1923 in a small village called Solotvino in Ruthenia in eastern Czechoslovakia (hence the later sobriquet of 'the bouncing Czech') into a poverty-stricken Jewish family. He was to change his name a number of times as well as his age, religion and nationality. Jan was born naturally left-handed but was made to write with his right hand when at school because the first characteristic was considered to be a sign of moral degeneracy. He read voraciously and had an almost uniquely retentive memory.

I wrote a polite letter to Stuart Errington explaining my decision to leave Mercantile Credit only to receive a rather abrupt response from a board director saying Mr Errington was ill and the matter would have to wait. I replied by giving my leaving date. I was invited into the director's dining room on my last day with the Finance House. I sat around the circular table and listening to their mostly banal conversation. One director was treasurer of Harlequins Rugby Football Club and they were agreeing the guest list for the next international at Twickenham. The strawberry pavlova was served but that was enough. I stood up, thanked them for their hospitality, returned to my office for the last time, shook a few hands and walked slowly up Southampton Row towards Euston Station. In the Bloomsbury area I met a group of Scottish football supporters who had arrived to go to Wembley to watch the international match the next day. One turned and slapped me around the head but, being out-numbered (where was Nigel Horton when you needed him?), I hurried on. I did however recall the words of Hamish Scott at Heathrow Airport:

"I dinna know much about ye Drury but I'm no impressed."

I arrived home to discover that Joyce, my mother-in-law, had arrived. Judy was in bed with suspected bronchitis and invaluable help had appeared. She was simply wonderful, looking after the naughty Christopher and the playful Emma.

Later in the evening I was working in my study when there was knock at my door (!). In came my mother-in-law. She reassured me that Judy would be fine and she thought that our two children were perfectly behaved. She then said that she would like to ask me a question.

"Tony, who is Robert Maxwell?"

A good question. I was about to discover the terrifying answer.

*****

CHAPTER THREE
A DESCENT INTO THE
UNBELIEVABLE AND THE FINAL
JUDGEMENT

The judge at the Central Criminal Court of England and Wales, usually referred to as 'the Old Bailey' (after the street in which it stands) hammered his gavel on its block and brought the court to order. He instructed the prisoner to stand up.

"Anthony Charles Drury, you have been found guilty of the most heinous crime of obtaining a pecuniary advantage by deception contrary to section 15A of the Theft Act 1968. You set out to mislead the British Printing and Communication Company and its highly respected owner that you are an experienced publishing executive when in fact you are nothing more than a hire-purchase salesman." He paused and stared at the defendant. "I sentence you to an indefinite period of incarceration to be served in the third-floor office of the managing director of Waterlow Publishers for a minimum of ten hours a day with hard labour being non-negotiable. Take the prisoner down."

The prosecuting counsel, a tall, dark, weighty individual was making a note to instruct his secretary (the afternoon one) to tell Harrods, the elitist departmental store, to deliver to the judge six bottles of Dom Perignon. The defence bench, Judy, Christopher and Emma, were bemused by the harshness of the judge's verdict although Christopher was amusing himself by flicking paper darts at the jurors. They, to a person, were standing up, waving their court papers and cheering. Several resembled individuals more usually found on the tenth floor of Elizabethan House in Great Queen Street, the head office of Mercantile Credit.

*

It has probably needed a substantial part of a Brazilian rain forest to produce the pulp used to generate enough paper to enable a great number of commentators to write their books on the life and times of Robert Maxwell before and after his death in November 1991. This is in addition to hundreds (perhaps thousands) of newspaper and magazine articles, media documentaries and several television plays and films.

The one issue on which I feel able to make a comment is that Robert Maxwell had a phenomenal understanding of the elixir of money. In my own case, by doubling my salary he made me captive to his behest. I was not worth his hubris but I suspect he already knew the value I could bring to his business activities as I will reveal below. I watched him striding the corridors of power in the City attracting around him individuals who added value to his empire and who, often, were tempted by the remuneration being offered. The clever ingredient, Maxwell at his brilliant best, was that unlike most moguls who believe money does all the talking, Captain Bob added personal status. I could not wait to start dictating letters to my secretary which had at the bottom in bold lettering, 'A C Drury, Managing Director, Waterlow Publishers Limited.' I sent them to several directors of Mercantile Credit for the flimsiest of reasons. I did not care. I was the coming man. My father studied the BPCC balance sheet and financial accounts and sent me a list of questions which I could not answer.

By recruiting individuals who had fallen down the greasy pole and redressing them with a position which reflected status and financial security, Robert Maxwell built a fortress around his empire. One of his adoring guards was the managing director of Waterlow Publishers who had left behind a middle-manager's position in an administration division of a finance house and become, overnight, a member of the management classes operating out of a public company which was attracting wave after wave of media headlines and comment. It was breath-taking.
Within weeks of starting work for the British Printing and Communication Company, my life had radically changed.

Rising at 5.30am I left Leighton Buzzard and drove south down the M1 onto the City Road into Finsbury Square and the car park adjacent to Worship Street where Maxwell House was situated and where I parked my new Audi 80 Quattro. I aimed to be at my desk on the third floor by 7.45am. There was a particular reason in that Maxwell controlled everything and, in particular, he personally signed all approval forms relating to staff employment, capital expenditure and expenses. I discovered that he was often available in his office before 8.00am and occasionally in a benign mood. My success rate was about forty per cent. At other times I drove out to Headington Hall in Oxford in an effort to see him. At around 6.00pm each working day I went to a pub in Finsbury Square, Finch's, and would mix with BPCC staff. The main and often only topic of conversation was Robert Maxwell. Individuals lived on their last contact with the Chairman: his aura was phenomenal. My departure time for the return journey home was between 7.00pm and 9.00pm. One night at the later time, as I was leaving, a taxi drew up outside the main entrance and two possibly Swedish hostesses alighted and asked the security guard for the way to Mr Maxwell's office.

Waterlow Publishers was an impressive company. Employing around one hundred and twenty staff, its range of products included books and magazines including 'Financial Weekly' in which the Chairman took a special interest. The company had a series of joint ventures including with a firm of leading chartered accountants where it published academic books under their sponsorship. There was a competent management structure and, for a majority of the time, the daily commitment lay outside the events taking place on the Chairman's floor. Waterlow Publishers was profitable and I had found a situation which was professionally fulfilling and where I felt I could make a contribution to the BPCC Group. My chairman Sam Silkin was supportive and offered helpful advice from time to time. On my third day there was a knock on my door and a scruffy person walked in. "I've come to tell you your odds," he said. When I asked him to

41

explain what he meant he continued, "The odds we are offering on you being sacked within three months." I smiled and told the intruder that this did not apply to me because I had been chosen personally by the Chairman. "That's what they all say," he preened. On hearing the odds being dangled I took a ten pounds bet on myself and made some useful money.

Whether or not I had seen the Chairman in the early morning, around coffee time my internal telephone would ring and a secretary would say, "Now, Tony!". Thereupon a ritual developed involving a summons to Maxwell's office, a rant from Maxwell and a list of tasks for me to undertake which he recalled the next day and always managed to ask about the one I had failed to complete. I had received a whisper in my ear that I was expected to attend the Chairman's dining room every day. It was extraordinary but on virtually all occasions important visitors were in attendance including politicians, City leaders and Services personnel. The cuisine was sumptuous except for Maxwell who always had a silver bowl filled with soft French cheeses and fresh grapes which he scooped out with his hand and gorged on.

On several occasions he told me to be at the entrance to Maxwell House where his dark red Rolls Royce was waiting. The registration number was PP 64, the year when he acquired Pergamon Press on which he initially built an academic publishing house which experienced a range of problems and was sold to the Dutch conglomerate Elsevier in March 1991. Maxwell was stopped frequently by the road traffic police when driving to and from Oxford and so he abandoned the practice and employed a chauffeur. I travelled in the Rolls perhaps four times and it was never the same driver because they were regularly sacked. Driving with him was a daunting experience because he undertook three tasks at the same time. He yelled at the chauffeur on which traffic lane to take, continually chiding the driver's choice, he took phone calls all the time and he lectured me on various topics not least his own success in life.

My mornings began to take on a new direction as I became friendly with Ian and Kevin Maxwell who invited me for coffee with them. They usually talked about one topic, their father. They were in awe and in fear in equal measure.

Five days a week I was owned by Robert Maxwell. He occasionally phoned me at the weekend and twice on a Saturday morning I met him at Headington Hall. It was the one area where I eventually resisted and he seemed to accept my wish. On Saturday mornings and to give Judy a rest I took Christopher and Emma to Stratford-upon-Avon to see my aging parents. In the evening we gave dinner parties and my status as managing director of Waterlow Publishers and the tales of Robert Maxwell (perhaps a little embellished, but not by much) made us engaging hosts. Then, into my life, came another global personality.

Tony, my dear chap, can I please borrow your office?

One day a person came into my office and sat down; he had an amazing presence about him – apart from being friendly, not always the case in Maxwell House. "The Chairman has told me to get to know you," he smiled and suggested we went for lunch together. As time went on, we were to share rather a lot of bottles of red wine necessitating the need on several occasions to book a hotel room for the evening to avoid the drink-drive traffic offence.

Peter Jay has been described as the golden boy of his generation. Educated at Winchester College and Christ Church College, Oxford where he gained a first-class honours degree in PPE (Philosophy, Politics and Economics), he became the economics editor of 'The Times', married Margaret Callaghan, the daughter of Labour politician James Callaghan who, three years later, became the prime minister. Peter was appointed British Ambassador in Washington; his wife had an affair with Watergate journalist Carl Bernstein (co-author of 'All the President's Men') and Peter had an affair with their children's nanny. He returned to the United Kingdom and joined BPCC as Robert Maxwell's chief of staff.

Every Tuesday Peter came into my office and stayed until lunchtime when we went to a local Italian restaurant and consumed, more often than not, two bottles of vino rosso. He was always polite and relaxed: we never discussed the Chairman or his time in Washington. He effectively taught me about economics and once he quoted from my book, 'Finance Houses' when he was explaining the complexities of financial regulation. From June 2003 until May 2009, he was a non-executive director of the Bank of England.

On one occasion he was later than usual and when he came in said, "Tony, dear chap, I have a great favour to ask of you. May I please borrow your office for an hour?" As I rose from behind my desk to vacate the room in walked the television host, journalist and writer David Frost (Sir David Frost OBE) who shook me by the hand and thanked me for making room for him. He died in 2013 at the age of 74. He has a memorial stone in Poet's Corner of Westminster Abbey.

On another occasion, and unusually for Peter, he arrived in a buoyant mood and, as he sat down, told me that he had just been with the Chairman and had told him what a splendid job I was doing as managing director of Waterlow Publishers. I groaned inwardly. Twenty minutes later my desk phone rang and a voice said, "Tony, come!" As I sat down in Maxwell's office I would not have been surprised if a Reginald Perrin squeaker had emitted a loud blast. Maxwell was enraged, shouting at me and shaking his fist before telling me to go away albeit he used more colourful language.

Peter Jay left BPCC at the end of 1989 when he was told to go. In his book 'Fall: The Mystery of Robert Maxwell' author John Preston writes, 'Having spent the last three years being belittled, ridiculed and telephoned in the middle of the night, Jay was not unduly downhearted.' He is now 86. It was a privilege to have known him and share his company discussing economics in an Italian restaurant in Finsbury Square on a number of occasions.

Another Banking (World) Crisis. Call for Tony Drury

It was unusual for Eric Glover, the Secretary-General of the Institute of Bankers, to invite me out to lunch but, as we settled down at his table in a restaurant in Throgmorton Street, he immediately launched into a rant about Robert Maxwell. It took a starter of Brioche Crab Melts with truffle butter and a glass of Pinot Grigio to calm him down. He was being attacked from two sides: in the more civilised corner, his bosses at the Institute of Bankers and on the opposite side, Robert Maxwell. The Chairman was now not taking his calls. I had no idea what he was talking about. The answer was simple. The contract for the publishing of the newly created magazine 'Banking World' was not yet signed. A point of order flashed through my mind in that Peter Jay, who was supposed to be appointing the editor, never mentioned it to me albeit there was no specific reason he should do so.

There were three issues according to my now slightly calmer companion. The actual control of the magazine (it was not hard to work out Maxwell's position on that issue), the charges in that the Institute were paying BPCC for the work involved in publishing it and finally the cost of printing the magazine which Maxwell was insisting was undertaken by Waterlow Printers in Dunstable (a BPCC company but separate to Waterlow Publishers).

Early on in my BPCC career I was staggered to come back from lunch and find that the third floor of Maxwell House, where Waterlow Publishers was based, was occupied by perhaps thirty-five workers including three women. The staff were gathered at one end of the floor and the managers were perplexed as the shouting and somewhat coarse language dominated proceedings. I managed to identify a 'ringleader' and discovered that the administration offices of Waterlow Printers were situated on the floor above. The workers were demanding increased wages and had brought their case to the Chairman but had managed to occupy the wrong area. I asked that they move to the fourth floor only to receive a reply which, in their own way, suggested that was not the intention. I closed our offices and sent everyone home. At around 8.00pm Maxwell appeared bringing with him boxes of sandwiches and many bottles of beer. He was incredible as he asked the printers to gather around him. There was much jocularity and then the serious business started. At around midnight, the strike was over and the representatives of Waterlow Printers returned to Dunstable. I later ascertained that they managed to negotiate forty per cent of the increase they wanted: Maxwell then threatened, if they did not accept his 'final' offer, to close the company down: classical strategic negotiating because the leaders knew, if pushed, he would. They retired claiming a victory and Maxwell laughed to himself.

We discussed the matter and I asked Eric Glover who was pulling the strings at the Institute of Bankers. He said that was an easy question. It was (Sir) John Quinton who, in 1987, became chairman of Barclays Bank and who was the first chairman of the newly formed Football Association Premier League. It was John Quinton who had masterminded the Barclays Bank takeover of Mercantile Credit. I suggested to Eric that he meet with his effective master and ask him what was his bottom line on the matter. A week later the reply came that John Quinton just wanted the contract settled and signed and would (blank) Robert Maxwell just give way on at least one of the points of disagreement.

I caught the Chairman early one morning a few days later at around 7.30am and decided this was the best chance I might have.

"Chairman," I said, "I think that the Institute of Bankers are treating you disgracefully." Maxwell was interested. "The reason I am here today, Chairman, is because of your brilliance in creating 'Banking World.'" I was ahead on points. "And I think it is unacceptable that the Institute are not agreeing to the perfectly reasonable demands you are making, Chairman." I was still alive. "But I know these bankers: it's my world. Give them something, Chairman, to get the matter settled.

Maxwell stared at me. "And what do you suggest I give in on, Mr Drury?"

"The charges, Chairman, halve them."

I was wondering when my dismissal letter would arrive. Maxwell smiled. "I've doubled them anyway," he laughed.

"Go on," he continued, "tell your little friend Eric Glover that I'll discount the charges by forty per cent."

A week later, in the early evening, I boarded the Rolls and drove with the Chairman and Sam Silkin to the Institute of Bankers in the heart of the City. Maxwell was unusually quiet and treated the whole event with great seriousness. We were shown into the boardroom at the Institute, Maxwell and the chairman of the Institute gave brief speeches and the contract for the publishing of 'Banking World' was signed. John Quinton came over and shook my hand. In 1987 the organisation received the royal assent and became The Chartered Institute of Bankers.

As we were leaving after a glass of wine the Chairman took me to one side.

"Mr Drury," he said, "you are impressing a number of people. I am very pleased with you."

I drove home to Bedfordshire up the M1 motorway (I had limited myself to one glass of bubbly) elated and arrived home to tell Judy that I was increasing her allowance by thirty per cent and we were going on holiday to Portugal. Christopher and Emma were in disgrace because Judy was struggling to find babysitters for us due to their bombing with wet sponges of the last school girl willing to undertake the task.

But for Tony Drury, managing director of Waterlow

Publishers, that proved to be a minor distraction. Lying in wait was a slow-burning fuse leading to a stick of gelignite.

The 1983 signing of the 'Banking World' contract at the Institute of Bankers in London. From left to right: Eric Glover, the Secretary-General of the Institute; (Sir) John Quinton, Barclays Bank; the Chairman of the Institute, Robert Maxwell; Sam Silkin, Chairman, Waterlow Publishers; the author.

For the first time since joining BPCC I took a day off work due to the need to visit my mother who was in Warwick General Hospital following an operation. The weekend that followed was a festive time as I luxuriated in the words of the Chairman: "I am very pleased with you." On Monday I sprinted up the stairs of Maxwell House to try to meet with my boss before 8.00am but his office was locked. I tried to locate Ian and Kevin but the brothers were nowhere to be found. I spent the day preparing my presentation for the Tuesday budget meeting when the managing directors of the six publishing companies based in Worship Street explained their strategy for the coming year. On reflection there was a change in the atmosphere but I was focused on impressing the Chairman the following day.

Before then, later in the afternoon, there was a meeting with the Chairman and the senior staff of the Waterlow Publishers' title 'Financial Weekly' albeit it was, to all intents and purposes, a separate business. They were a committed and hard-working team but were struggling to increase sales and wanted a substantial promotional budget to be agreed by the Chairman. Maxwell arrived over one hour late and I began the presentation on behalf of the 'Financial Weekly' team. "Shut up," he said. He commenced a long rambling diatribe about what I have no idea and then took the editor into his office.

There was to be one benefit of this situation in that working for 'Financial Weekly' was a rather bright individual who was subsequently to reach the top of his journalistic profession. Since 1989, David Smith has been the Economics Editor of the 'Sunday Times' and writes a widely read feature each week on current political and financial matters. A few years ago we reconnected, he recalled my tussles with the Chairman and we have since shared a number of anecdotes about Robert Maxwell.

Tuesday came, my mother was recovering and I drove down the M1 to work in high spirits. I tried to gain access to Maxwell's office but his secretary, making an early start, said he was not available. I found Ian in his office but as I approached him, he closed his door. The budget meeting was scheduled to start at 9.00am and we all assembled in the boardroom. The Chairman came in at 10.20am and announced that he was changing the order of proceedings and Waterlow Publishers would go first. "Great," I whispered under my breath. My presentation was Tony Drury at his best and the eight minutes I took (bearing in mind Maxwell's short-term attention span) was word perfect. Maxwell glowered at me and instructed that I should follow him into his office. The truth was beginning to dawn on me. From my 'Reggie Perrin' chair I looked up at him and realised that he seemed nervous.

"Mr Drury," he said, "what have you achieved for me

as managing director of Waterlow Publishers?" I summarised the presentation I had just made in the boardroom in front of all my colleagues.

"I want you to go to Headington Hall and run one of my other publishing companies," he said in a subdued voice. My mind went back to the signing of the 'Banking World' contract at the Institute of Bankers which I now realised was also the signing of my own death warrant. I stared at Maxwell and burst out laughing. I cannot explain why that happened. I tried to recapture the grovelling verbosity which had landed me my job in the first place but even I didn't believe what I was saying.

"Are you saying "no" to me, Mr Drury?" asked the Chairman.

I was overtaken by an overwhelming sense of fear and disappointment because I was not prepared to move to Headington Hall. I nodded my head. Maxwell looked at me and spoke his final words.

"You're no fucking good," he said. "Get out of my office."

I wandered back to my desk and it was clear that Maxwell had prepared the ground: there was total silence from my staff. An hour later the finance director came to see me and we agreed the terms of my departure. My contract of employment was to be paid in full and I would be given a favourable reference. I was to be allowed to keep my Audi 80 Quattro for four weeks and then I was to return it. He asked when I wanted to actually leave the company, I suggested "now" and he agreed. I tried to see Sam Silkin but he was not available. Peter Jay had been spotted but had left the building a little after 10.30am. I tidied my desk, shook a few hands and left the office to begin the journey back to Leighton Buzzard. I simply had no idea how I was going to explain these events to Judy, Christopher and Emma. In truth, I could not explain them to myself.

The family were great, albeit Judy asked how were we going to pay the bills. I was devastated not because I knew others, certainly at Mercantile Credit, would be relishing my demise, but because I wanted to keep the position of managing director of Waterlow Publishers. I discovered that the day after I left BPCC, Kevin Maxwell took over from me.

In July 1984, Maxwell, with the help of his London banking friends, took over the Mirror Group of Newspapers incorporating the 'Daily Mirror', the 'Sunday Mirror' and the 'Sunday People'. In 1991 he sailed his yacht up Manhattan's East River, conquered New York and, using money he did not have, bought the ailing tabloid the 'New York Daily News'. On the fifth of November of the same year, he was alone (apart from the crew) on his boat off the Canary Islands near to the coast of south-west Spain when, at the age of 68, he jumped into the ocean to commit suicide. The truth of his precarious financial position quickly became known and far too many Mirror pensioners lost some or even all of their retirement funds.

Reflections

In the extraordinary life and times of Robert Maxwell my involvement was but a pinprick. Others, better placed, have made their judgements and usually condemned him, some in vitriolic terms. I joined him at a moment when his status was absolutely at its peak. He was a master of media manipulation and relished his battles with his Australian rival Rupert Murdoch. When we went to the Institute of Bankers to sign the 'Banking World' contract he was welcomed into their offices with an almost regal affection. In my time at Maxwell House, I watched the good and the great of the City queue to have time with him and secure huge fees from BPCC. Later they were the same professionals who condemned him for his wickedness. A few had their doubts and gave Robert Maxwell a miss. But, in truth, very few.

My time with Captain Bob exploded my own ambition and my difficulty in accepting public school corporate governance such as I had experienced at Mercantile Credit.

Whatever the truth, he was always entertaining. Long after his demise the stories about him proliferated and one of my favourites was when one day, he was due at Barclays Bank for a lunchtime gathering. He phoned his host and said, "Julian, it's Bob here. I'm over Paris in my helicopter and won't make your event." The reply came, "That's a pity, Bob, because the Governor of the Bank of England has just arrived." Says Maxwell, "I'll be round in five minutes."

The story of my time with Robert Maxwell would not be complete without mention of a rather beautiful, dark-haired young woman. In the next chapter I will be explaining my experiences with three rather sensational ladies.

****

CHAPTER FOUR
BEAUTY IS IN THE EYE OF THE BEHOLDER: THE STORIES OF THREE 'PERFECT' WOMEN

'She was a phantom of delight
When first she gleam'd upon my sight;
A lovely apparition, sent
To be a moment's ornament;
Her eyes as stars of twilight fair;
Like twilight's, too, her dusky hair;
But all things else about her drawn
From May-time and the cheerful dawn,
A dancing shape, an image gay,
To haunt, to startle, and waylay.'

In 1804 William Wordsworth wrote this poem dedicated to his wife Mary Hutchinson: it was called the 'Perfect Woman'. I must declare an interest. As previously mentioned, I have been married for fifty-four years and Judy is still the amazing blonde who I 'discovered' when she was working for the manager at Midland Bank, Kidderminster and from whom I 'stole' her.

Uxorious poetry can be found elsewhere in English literature. John Milton, in 'Paradise Lost', wrote:

'By that uxorious being whose heart, though large,
Beguiled by fair idolatresses,
Fell to idols foul.'

In the City, the third century BC (BCE) Greek proverb 'Beauty is in the eye of the beholder' probably reflects more accurately the male approach to women.

Shakespeare in 'Love's Labour Lost', written in 1588, wrote:

'Beauty is bought by judgement of the eye,
Not utter'd by base sale of chapman's tongues.'

Beauty is not limited to a geographical area or sector, albeit politics seems to generate some beguiling individuals as I will be exampling in the third part of this chapter. Women working in the City were attracted by the combination of wealth, power and status and some knew exactly how to maximise the opportunities available to them particularly while their 'enchantment' was irresistible.

On the tenth floor of Elizabethan House, in Great Queen Street, not far from Holborn Tube Station, the directors of Mercantile Credit had their offices and their staff. Unbeknown to them, the ladies ranked their bosses in terms of 'sex appeal' and booking Friday night hotel rooms was a bonus for the most promiscuous secretaries.

Occasionally, in fact very occasionally, a woman came along who had all the attributes referred to above and then the extra 'X' factor. Perhaps President John Kennedy would have called it the 'Marilyn Monroe' seduction or Prime Minister John Major, the 'Edwina Currie' exertions (she did call him a 'sexy beast'). It was the ability to make men lose their self-control and, in the case of the second subject of this chapter, large amounts of their money. There are three women who I encountered in my time in the City who for me, and many others, had the X factor.

There was, however, another aspect of working with females in the 'City' and that was: never to rush to judgement. Some years later, in 2013, when working in the corporate finance sector, I was part of an after-work drinks party in a London Wall pub. As the alcohol took effect the conversation turned to the latest publishing sensation: E L James had written a trilogy which began with 'Fifty Shades of Grey' telling of the relationship between college graduate Anastasia Steele and youthful business magnate Christian Grey. The erotic scenes of sexual practices included bondage, dominance and masochism. The boyish attitude in the group was leading to some fairly loutish behaviour.

Within the group was a corporate lawyer whose role was to vet the documents produced when introducing companies to the various stock markets. She was rather attractive but known to be married with two children. One of the 'boys' made a comment in her direction asking if she was a fan of Anastasia? Megan exploded:
`"Don't you ever mention that book or that woman in my presence again," she yelled. "My husband and I are dedicated to raising our family in an atmosphere of honesty and decency." She stood up. "We do not do 'filth'," Megan concluded as she stormed out of the hostelry.

Those remaining were stunned and it was clear that Megan had earned their respect with her stance against overt promiscuity. There was just one contradiction to the incident. I knew, because he had told me, that Megan was having an affair with a colleague of mine, a criminal barrister, based in Lincoln's Inn Fields. Every two weeks she told her husband that she was staying overnight in London because a transaction was completing and she could not be sure of the timings. My squash partner confidant also told me that Megan made Anastasia Steele seem more of a beginner when it came to bedroom athletics.

"Tony. I do hope that you'll be coming to my father's party"

Early in my tenure as managing director of Waterlow Publishers I was walking amongst the workstations of around one hundred and twenty staff when the manager who was guiding me pointed to a desk where there was sitting a dark-haired young woman. I went up to her, said who I was and asked if she was enjoying her work. She looked up at me and smiled.

Ghislaine Noelle Marion Maxwell, who was born in France on Christmas Day, 1961, the ninth and youngest of the Maxwell siblings, was part way through a modern history with languages degree at Balliol College, Oxford University and was learning the work of a book editor. She graduated in 1985. In June 2021 she was found guilty of sex trafficking in conjunction with the then deceased sex offender Jeffrey Epstein and who, in June 2022, was sentenced by a New York court to twenty years' imprisonment which she is serving in a mixed-sex facility, the Federal Correctional Institute, Tallahassee in Florida. She is currently appealing her sentence.

I melted as she radiated a personality and friendliness which was breath-taking. She had an inner confidence and a certainty of knowing the rules. She thanked me for my question and replied that she was enjoying her work and learning a great deal. In response to my next comment, she told me about her university course. She then said how impressed she was with the company and asked me if I was pleased with the work of the staff? I moved on but made certain I revisited her desk on several future occasions. During our second chat I suggested that she should feel able to come to my office if there was any way in which I could help her. She thanked me and we moved on.

About a month later there was knock at my door and in came Ghislaine. After accepting my invitation to take a seat, she reminded me of what I had said and she asked for my help. I ordered coffee for the two of us and she explained that she was editing a book on banking and had come across the term 'secondary banks' and she did not fully understand it. We discussed the implications of her question and I wondered if I should refer her to my book on finance houses ...perhaps not. She thanked me and said she must get back to her work. As she was leaving, she turned and said:

"I do hope, Mr Drury, that I'll be seeing you at my father's party?"

Robert Maxwell was organising an event at Headington Hall with the precision of a military operation. I was told to submit a list of twenty guests from Waterlow Publishers. Each submission was returned with his scrawl all over it. On one he had written something which, as far as I could decipher, suggested I did not know anyone important. I did not reach his reception because he had terminated my employment and so I never again met his daughter.

Ghislaine has attracted almost as much publicity as her late father, mainly through her relationship with American financier and convicted sex-offender Jeffrey Epstein. He was involved in a number of business transactions with Robert Maxwell and it is thought by some commentators that following his suicide, Epstein became Ghislaine's surrogate father as well as an occasional lover. She is tarnished with her sex offences conviction but I do wonder about the list of names in her to date undisclosed 'little black book'. It has been reported in the national press that 'she had two US presidents, a Pope and A-lister celebrities on speed-dial on her phone.' Based on my brief experiences with her at Maxwell House I sense that the visitors to Epstein's homes were equally seduced by the beauty and mesmeric presence of Ghislaine. For sure, she knew how to use her talents.

These came to the surface in the early stages of her sentence in the Florida prison. Ghislaine, now 61, began running courses for other inmates in which she taught the three principles of etiquette: focusing on honesty, consideration and respect. They have proved popular partly because the training counts towards the First Step Act allowing inmates to reduce their sentences by up to fifteen days. Her message was said, by a fellow prisoner, to be, 'if you are a woman and a convicted felon, you're not a second-class citizen.'

She, however, seems unable to avoid controversy. In January 2023 Ghislaine appeared on the UK's TalkTV in a taped interview with Jeremy Kyle during which she complained about the conditions in which she was being held. This resulted in her being temporarily secured in the Special Housing Unit where inmates are locked away for up to twenty-three hours a day in a tiny cell and fed through slits in the door.

"Would you like to conquer the world, Tony?" her eyes asked me.

During my time in the City no other woman managed the 'X' factor with the accomplishment of the entrepreneur sitting in the boardroom at St Helen's Capital, the corporate finance business I founded a number of years after leaving Robert Maxwell.

My lunch at the Institute of Chartered Accountants had over-run and I was late for a client presentation which was being organised by my fellow director. I had no knowledge of the proposal but that was not unusual. The early times with potential clients were spent trying to assess them and their proposition and I was impressed that my colleague had assembled our best sales team to meet with the visitor and her advisers. I had been told that the introduction had been made by a firm of solicitors well known to us.

If I achieved anything during my time building up St Helen's Capital it was gaining the intuitive ability to assess our potential clients. Despite our protestations, many arrived with the expectation that we were going to hand them a cheque. The minimum period of time between first meeting the potential customer and completing their transaction was three months and more usually, six to nine months. This was because the regulatory environment was demanding (much more so now because of the numbers of frauds and cases of duplicity) and due to the rather sensible 'built-in' check that the process itself determined if boards of directors and their businesses were suited to the rigours of a market listing. Nearly always I would focus on the chief executive officer (often the founder of the business) and the finance director because they were more often than not the two driving forces behind the company.

Occasionally, my 'intuition' was found wanting. We were three days into a series of client presentations involving a Yorkshire-based chemicals company and London equity and institutional investors and our morale was buoyant as we neared raising the full amount of funds required. The chief executive was impressive but it was the finance director who took the plaudits. She had prepared her own presentation of the financial information, rather thoughtfully, with each slide containing a headline message. Her second tactic was that she did not say very much; she let the figures do the talking. To be honest her own statistics turned a few heads but this was serious work and her professionalism was impressing several of the City operators we were meeting. The final presentation, to be made at our offices to the managers of a pension fund – and perhaps the most important because our head of sales had already obtained a tentative agreement from them to make a significant investment – was at nine o'clock in the morning. Whereupon, we could not find the two clients. In an atmosphere of some concern, we dispatched a member of staff to their hotel. She returned with an envelope addressed to me. It was actually a rather beautiful letter. The chief executive explained that he and Daphne (the finance director) had, over the last few months, resisted the growing temptation to become personally involved but a long train journey and three nights together in London (they were staying at the Bloomsbury Hotel) proved to be the pivotal moment in their relationship: they had told their families and were going to live in New Zealand. The business would be sold. My finance director blamed me for taking on a transaction which yielded no fees to St Helen's Capital. I said I would brush up on my marriage guidance skills. But now it was time to assess another potential customer.

Our offices in St Helen's Place, which is owned by the Leathersellers' Company, not far from the Bank of England, created a good impression on our visitors. I joined the meeting and sat at the end of the table because I did not want to interrupt proceedings. The visiting entrepreneur locked her eyes on me and I knew immediately that her advisers would have told her who made the decisions at St Helen's Capital. She was seated but I was able to assess her fair hair, clear facial skin, and eyes which were hypnotic. The briefing notes told me that she was twenty-seven years of age.

To my surprise, and to that of the whole room, she stopped talking, stood up and said that she wanted to tell Mr Drury about her product, which she did. It was dynamically impressive. She then picked up her file of papers and announced that she had to leave for another meeting and St Helen's Capital had twenty-four hours to decide whether they wanted to join her journey which she said would see her conquer the world. As she was leaving, she shook me by the hand and squeezed my fingers.

My colleague took care of the departure and then we all sat down in the boardroom and the sales team was in overdrive. This wasn't just 'a deal', it was potentially a business-changing moment. After a few minutes a silence descended and everybody looked at me. I asked my colleague to join me in my office where I closed the door. He was on cloud nine, but only briefly, because I told him we were not going to be involved. To be fair he held his composure and asked me why? I explained that I knew the solicitor who was advising the entrepreneur and he was on a blacklist well known to the City regulators. When he asked how I had come across this explosive information I told him that it was my job to know these things. The sales team did what sales teams do: they moved on to the next deal.

Watching events unfurl as the entrepreneur took the financial world by storm has been interesting because I would never have guessed that her product did not work. I can clearly remember her squeezing my fingers. I was with her for no more than twenty minutes. Some 'X' factor!

Described by Forbes magazine as 'the world's youngest self-made female billionaire', Elizabeth Anne Holmes was born on the third of February 1984 in Washington DC and was described as a polite but withdrawn child: her parents were bureaucrats on Capitol Hill. At the age of nine she wrote a letter to her father saying she wanted to discover something new. In 2002 she went to Stanford University to study chemical engineering, dropping out after one year. She had already come up with a medical patch that could scan the wearer for infections.

She launched Theranos which created a way of

testing blood from a simple finger prick and attracted investors who had not even seen any financial information. Her backers included US Treasury Secretary George Schultz and media tycoon (and arch rival of Robert Maxwell) Rupert Murdoch. At its height Theranos was valued at £6.5billion. Elizabeth Holmes numbered former US President Bill Clinton as a supporter.

In 2015, a whistle-blower raised concerns about the testing results published by the company, a story followed by 'The Wall Street Journal'; lawsuits resulted, her partners evaporated and in 2016 US regulators banned Holmes from operating a blood-testing service for two years. In 2018, Theranos was dissolved and Holmes settled civil charges from the regulators that she had fraudulently raised $700m from investors. Three months later she was arrested on criminal charges of wire fraud. In January 2022 she failed in an attempt to flee the US by government officials after buying a one-way ticket to Mexico. Her business partner, Ramesh 'Sunny' Balwani, with whom she had been romantically involved, was convicted of twelve counts of fraud and sentenced to thirteen years in prison. On 18 November 2022 she was sentenced to 135 months in prison for defrauding investors.

In 2019 Elizabeth Holmes reportedly married William 'Billy' Evans, heir to the Evans Hotel group in San Diego. They had a baby son and then a second child, both born after she was indicted on criminal fraud and conspiracy charges in 2018. Her legal team is arguing that her family ties mean she is not a flight risk and that she should be allowed to remain free while she appeals her convictions.

"I want to be rich. Get me into here."

In the year 2005 the political fortunes of the Conservative party and the profitability of my corporate finance house were moving in opposite directions.

The Labour political maestro Tony Blair had secured a third term in office in the May General Election when winning 412 seats against the Conservative Michael Howard's 166 and the Liberal Democrat Charles Kennedy's 51. Conservative party members were in total despair after years of Labour's dominance.

I was later to dine with Michael Howard when the Blue Dragons, mentioned below, were seeking a new chairman following the death of (Lord) Peter Walker. We met at a restaurant which describes itself as a 'Bastion of Britishness': 'Wiltons' in Jermyn Street in St James is a favourite of Conservative members and creates a 'privileged' atmosphere in its exclusive dining areas. Michael was always a 'fill-in' following the departure of Iain Duncan Smith but I gained the impression that he gave the leadership role everything he possessed. However, Tony Blair was unassailable at that period in the UK's political fortunes.

For St Helen's Capital the outlook was different, with buoyant stock markets and overseas companies coming to the City to take advantage of investors' appetite for Chinese growth companies and East Asian oil and mineral businesses.

My own political commitment was growing and I had become the leader of the Blue Dragons who were Welsh Conservatives working in London, on the basis of having a Welsh mother-in-law, a half-Welsh wife and a holiday home in Aberdovey. I was interested in a pair of aspiring and youthful contenders for power. David Cameron and George Osborne had brains and policies and I invited St Helen's contacts to the evening drinks parties that they attended. Through another channel I had become friendly with Norman (Lord) Lamont, the former cabinet minister and had 'advised' him not to invest in a share which I knew was being touted in the City.

A year after becoming Member of Parliament for Witney, David Cameron became a special adviser to Norman Lamont, the Chancellor of the Exchequer. At a later date, the now former minister agreed to be guest of honour at one of the City lunches which St Helen's Capital periodically held. He was in excellent form and held his audience's attention with his telling of Treasury stories. However, in the small talk that followed, he picked up that a certain individual was associated with our company. He stood up, walked out and never spoke to me again. The individual in question had been romantically involved with Lord Lamont's wife. Even my finance director could not blame me for that one!

It was approaching the autumn of 2005 and Michael Howard had resigned as the party leader. The battle for succession ended up between David Cameron and David Davis and I sensed that party morale was on the upward path, not least because Tony Blair and Gordon Brown were involved in an unpleasant dispute over their 'Granita agreement' where Blair promised to hand over the premiership to Brown after one term and then changed his mind. They were also at odds over joining the Euro currency. Blair was an arch Europhile and media speculation was that he saw himself as a future president of the European Union. Brown was obdurately against the surrender of the pound sterling and determined to ensure that it never happened.

I visited the office of my finance director at St Helen's Capital and said that I was going to take a table at the Conservative Westminster Ball. The ten seats at £500 a time plus wines and carriages would total around £6,000. He had apoplexy which is what finance directors do. I was yet to tell him that he was not included on the guest list. The event is essentially a fund-raising opportunity. Political parties are always raising money and one of Donald Trump's pathways to his US presidential victory in 2017 was because he attracted a vast war-chest from rich Americans and corporations who wanted to join his crusade to make America great again.

The Conservative Party was fundamentally well financed and adroit at securing business patronages. A respected senior member of parliament told me that granting a peerage was similar to writing out a cheque for a million pounds if the fees, pensions and other opportunities are aggregated. The Campaign Headquarters inner circle wanted an improved financial base on which to fight the next general election and the Westminster Ball was a key moment in their strategic planning. It was not just the sale of tickets, tombola and auction which produced the funding: it was the furtive conversations and introductions which really mattered.

After booking our table I consulted widely on the guest list as I wanted it to work in our best interests. The invitations were issued and there was a hundred per cent acceptance. There was my founding fellow director, seven rather wealthy and influential individuals (a senior lawyer, American banker, 'top five' accountant, a Chinese entrepreneur and several seriously rich investors) plus myself; there was room for one more. There is a tradition that a 'table' can invite a Conservative member of parliament to join them and it is virtually mandatory that the individual accepts. My choice emailed me within hours of receiving her post. The 'X' factor was delighted to accept.

The atmosphere on the evening was pulsating partly due to the quality of the champagne being served but mainly because of the news that the leadership battle was over, regardless of the process still to be enacted. The electoral messiah was on his way: son of a London stockbroker who made pots of money, Eton, Oxford, handsome, with vitality and personality, a beautiful wife, Samantha, daughter of a baronet and Viscountess Lady Astor, a young family and an adoring party membership. David Cameron was arriving. All it needed to make the evening a complete success was a princess. St Helen's Capital could not quite manage that but came fairly close to the task. She was on her way, late, by design no doubt, but even she gasped as she arrived and realised that her audience for the evening was dripping with wealth.

"Oh David, what a lovely surprise."

She was wearing a chiffon, off-the-shoulder, split lace evening dress and holding a designer handbag. I made the introductions and invited her to sit down but she was already working the table with her eyes. There was, almost immediately, only one focus of my guests' attention and she managed to maintain that for virtually the whole of the four hours we were all together. I reflected later that she must have spoken to my bank manager and discovered the state of my overdraft because I did not seem to register on her target list. We managed one conversation late on and that was interesting as she displayed her awareness of social issues troubling society. But, for now, there were other matters to which she turned her unbelievable charisma.

Nadine Vanessa Dorries (nee Bargery) was born in Liverpool in May 1957. Perhaps no other female politician (apart from Margaret (Lady) Thatcher) has courted as much attention and controversy as she was to achieve. She was elected the Member of Parliament for Mid Bedfordshire in the May 2005 General Election and went on in 2009 to be tarnished (but never 'convicted') in

67

the MPs' expenses scandal. In 2012 she described David Cameron and George Osborne as "two arrogant posh boys", in the same year she lost the party whip as a result of appearing in 'I'm a Celebrity, Get Me Out Of Here'; it was reinstated a year later. From September 2021 until the same month a year later, she was Secretary for State for Digital, Culture, Media and Sport, often at odds with BBC bosses, and led the case for the defence in support of Boris Johnson who was rejected by a majority of Conservative MPs as Prime Minister. She has written sixteen books to mixed editorial reviews.

The evening progressed and our table reverberated with enjoyment until the dessert plates were cleared away, coffee, port and brandy were served and David Cameron gave a speech. He spoke with courtesy, offering his defeated opponent David Davis praise, paying tribute to his predecessor Michael Howard and, cleverly, promised nothing. He emphasised the task ahead and correctly anticipated the close result coming in the next general election. The leader the Conservative Party had been waiting for arrived that evening and the applause went on and on, led by an 'X' factor member of our table.

Our guests settled down again and I knew that St Helen's Capital was having a productive evening. But I could not have anticipated what then happened. He had arrived at our table! David Cameron was working the floor. Nadine almost took off as she rushed up to his side. "Oh David, what a lovely surprise," she sang. He then kissed her cheek. Heaven had arrived for the Member of Parliament as the cameras flashed and our guests were photographed with DC. The Chinese entrepreneur managed to pose with David and Nadine: quite a coup.

The evening came to an end, business cards were exchanged, Nadine filled her appointments diary and my fellow director congratulated me on the success of the event. I was late leaving because I had to deal with a Blue Dragons (the Welsh Conservatives in London) matter and I realised, as I walked up the drive away from the dining hall, I was following David and Samantha Cameron.

They were arm in arm. I thought about speaking to them but there were to be more opportunities in the future. There were no obvious security guards. They walked on into political turmoil and eventually the Brexit referendum when the prime minister went to bed thinking he had won the Remain vote; he hadn't and, shortly afterwards, resigned.

As for our guest at the St Helen's table, I never again met Nadine Dorries. I would however confirm that, in my opinion, she had the 'X' factor that evening at the Westminster Ball.

When I arrived home in the early hours, Judy asked me what I thought of Nadine.

"Bit ordinary," I lied.

In February 2023 Nadine Dorries was once again where she yearned to be – in the newspapers making the headlines It was announced that she was to host a talk show 'Friday Night With Nadine' on TalkTV. She was accused by the Parliamentary anti-corruption watchdog of breaking the Ministerial Code by not consulting it before taking on the new role. No further action was taken. She used her television show to announce that she will not be standing as a member of parliament at the next general election.

Is there room for me?

Late in the preparation of this chapter a case for inclusion came from the antics of a lady who, until recently, gorged on self-publicity often by showing photographs of herself on social media wearing tantalising bikinis. It is no surprise that she attracted the sobriquet Baroness Bra.

Michelle Georgina Mone, Baroness Mone OBE (nee Allan) was born in October 1971 in Glasgow's East End. She set up the lingerie company Ultimo amongst her various businesses which included naturopathic 'weight-loss' pills and a cryptocurrency venture called Equi Capital which was forced to return investors' subscriptions and was described by the 'Financial Times' as a 'fiasco'.

In August 2015, the Prime Minister David Cameron, mentioned above when greeting Nadine Dorries at the Westminster Ball, made Michelle Mone, inexplicably in some people's opinion, a Conservative life peer. It is not known whether the former prime minister ever considered that Michelle Mone possessed the 'X' factor.

From 2020 to 2022, a series of investigative press articles reported that she and her children had secretly received, in an off-shore trust, £29million of profits (through an associated company PPE Medpro which she had promoted) from government PPE (Personal Protection Equipment) contracts during the Covid-19 pandemic. The House of Lords Commissioner for Standards and the National Crime Agency have launched their own investigations into the possible breaches of the law.

On 19 December 2022, the Government announced that it is suing PPE Medpro for £122 million plus costs. The matter is being contested by the directors of the company. In December 2022, Baroness Mone announced that she was taking leave of absence from the House of Lords.

*****

CHAPTER FIVE
"IF YOU WANT SOMETHING SAID, ASK A MAN; IF YOU WANT SOMETHING DONE, ASK A WOMAN."

Robert Maxwell created the opportunity for me to finance a publishing business by paying in full my contract. His influencing of news headlines, however, was overtaken by perhaps the most fearsome woman I ever met. The speaker of the above words, Margaret Thatcher, a barrister by training, Conservative Member of Parliament for Finchley from 1959 to 1990, was the Prime Minister of the United Kingdom from 1979 to 1990. She had a quality I have rarely seen replicated in any other person. It was her intensity, facial and physical, in whatever circumstance she found herself. Every word she spoke mattered.

In 2018, Judy and I went to The Alexandra, Birmingham's premier theatre, to watch the American songwriter Burt Bacharach who was touring the UK as part of his ninetieth birthday celebrations. The warm-up acts were good but nothing prepared us for the arrival on stage of the maestro. He played the piano for nearly two hours.

After a time, he settled into a routine of playing one of his seventy-three US hits and then chatting to the audience. One anecdote brought the house down. In his carefully crafted American speaking tone of voice, he told the story about his song, 'Raindrops Keep Falling on My Head':

"They said they wanted my song for a film," he drawled (it was 'Butch Cassidy and the Sundance Kid'). "I was not happy." He played a few bars of the music. "They told me it was about two Wild West outlaws," he said playing a few more notes. "I was very unhappy." He hit some more keys. "They turned it into a hit. I was very happy!" and then he played the whole song.

Towards the end Bacharach recalled that he was often asked what was the secret of his composing. He said to us that the answer was simple. "Every word, every note matters," and he then played and sang, "This Guy's in Love with You." He died aged 94 on 9 February 2023.

Whether Margaret Thatcher was aware of his dictum is not known but for her, like Bacharach, every word was important. Each thought was digested, opponents were demolished and her single-mindedness created the legend that remains in the history books. Long after she had left Westminster, I attended a London 'think tank' evening where she was due to speak; it had been sold out for weeks before. Now frail, and with John Major's government heading for an election abyss, she shuffled into the room, accelerated up to the front, turned and fixed her gaze on her followers. There was an explosion of emotion as their love and affection engulfed the more usual Conservative reserve. The 'Iron Lady' was with them and they relived the golden years, savouring her every word. She was too weak to stay for drinks and was led out to her waiting car. I never saw her again.

In 1982, at the time of the Falklands War, when Argentina tried to annex British territory in the South Atlantic Ocean, she was showing in the opinion polls as the most unpopular prime minister of all time. Her unyielding resolve as the British fleet took eight weeks to cover eight thousand nautical miles setting out from Plymouth in April to when Major General Jeremy Moore accepted the Argentinian forces surrender seventy-four days later, led her to become a national heroine.

Two years later, the Prime Minister clashed with the coalminers, led by the President of the National Union of Mineworkers, Arthur Scargill, across the country and her use of the Metropolitan Police, who attempted to stop pickets preventing strike-breakers from working, led to violent scenes.

For many, Margaret Thatcher's legacy was cemented in the 1984-1985 period of industrial strife and there are former colliery areas where she remains a detested figure. This was endorsed in the 1989/90 introduction of a Community Charge designed to replace the rating system used to fund local government. The Poll Tax was first introduced in Scotland and virtually wiped out support for the Conservatives to this day. Poll Tax riots took place across Great Britain until it was abolished.

"The problem with Socialism is that you eventually run out of other people's money."

This remains at the heart of what Margaret Thatcher said and believed. The concept of 'monetarism', called by some 'Thatcherism', was her real mission from long before she took the highest office. The Prime Minister's belief was that the United Kingdom needed to reduce state interventions, champion free markets and use low taxation to encourage entrepreneurism.

A new word entered the popular political lexicon: 'privatisation'. By 1990, more than forty state-owned businesses employing around 600,000 people, had been sold off. The sale in 1982 of the National Freight Company to its workers, led by (Sir) Peter Thompson, started the process but it was the Government-sponsored sale of major industries including British Airways, British Telecom, British Steel, British Gas and the water and rail industries which caught the headlines. The concept of private share ownership caught the public imagination.

Hey Jude, let's use your middle name!

Watching Mr Maxwell's pay-off disappear at an alarming rate spurred me on to start my first business venture. I knew, before the Chairman suggested I leave his office, what I was going to undertake. I wanted to build my own

Waterlow Publishers. It was a great business: I had hoped to survive the BPCC challenges, now it was time to do it myself. Hey Mrs Thatcher, I'm an entrepreneur!

We gave a dinner party to some friends and I was praying that they were not aware that the meal was accompanied by some rather cheap Spanish wine as we tried to work within a budget. The alcoholic banter focused on my new venture and I was asked a rather difficult question: "What is the name of your new company?" This led to an interesting exchange of views and our neighbour suggested 'Rushmere' which was the name of a local parkland area. That generated applause and so I opened another bottle of Rioja.

It was then decided that Rushmere Publishers was boring and it needed something with more impact. To the rescue rode Mrs Drury clutching her glass of wine. Judith Wynne Drury. 'Wynne' was her mother's maiden name. The right name for a publishing company and a tick in the box from my mother-in-law. Rushmere Wynne was born that night.

Within a year we had built up to ten titles about finance. I was aware of the developing governmental privatisation programme and managed to convince Michael Walters, the deputy city editor of the 'Daily Mail', to write 'How to make a killing in penny shares'. We appointed an agent to sell our books into retail outlets but it was hard work. Several brave investors supplemented our capital base and I took offices in a room above the local squash club, 'The Knolls'. Then I won an important game of golf, a rare event.

ProShare is created, and that's just the start

There was press comment that the Government, the London Stock Exchange and several City sponsors were creating an organisation to encourage wider share ownership. Two names caught my imagination: first, that of

Sir John Harvey-Jones MBE, chairman of Imperial Chemical Industries (ICI) from 1982 to 1987 and the mastermind behind the BBC series 'Trouble-shooter' when Sir John visited ailing businesses and advised the owners and directors how to weather the storms they were facing. With his unkempt and long hair, he was a viewers' favourite.

The second person mentioned was Sir Peter Thompson who had masterminded the 1982 sale of the National Freight Company, the first Government privatisation under the Thatcher mandate, to its workers. The shares were listed on the London Stock Exchange in 1989 and created some seriously wealthy shareholders.

I researched Sir Peter, discovered that he had offices in Bedfordshire and wrote to him expressing my interest at being involved with wider share ownership. He invited me to have coffee with him and we soon struck up a rapport. He was surprised when I asked if I could publish books and tender for the wider share ownership organisation's proposed magazine. He said he needed to think about that and suggested we play golf; we were both members at Woburn Golf Club. Two weeks later I sank a testing putt to claim victory on the eighteenth green of the Duke's course. We moved into the lounge where Sir Peter made me an offer. If I would agree to be the first director of private investor services at the new organisation, he would support my conditions – provided I base myself at the offices in Basinghall Street near to London's Guildhall.

It seemed to be a wonderful opportunity and my self-confidence was beginning to return following the Maxwell bruising. I was helped by a telephone call I received from a Mayfair-based firm of head-hunters who asked if I was interested in a banking position they were placing. I admitted rather sheepishly that I had been fired by Robert Maxwell.

"We understand that, Mr Drury," said the speaker. "Being sacked by Maxwell actually increases your value in the marketplace!"

Events moved steadily as Geoffrey Maddrell, an experienced industrialist, came into the wider share ownership organisation, as chief executive and staff were transferred from the London Stock Exchange. Sir John was a regular visitor and I remained in close contact with Sir Peter.

Why wider share ownership?

There were three main reasons why the Government's privatisation programme was so successful (leaving political arguments about the sale of state assets to one side). Firstly, the work of the Treasury was outstanding. The form-filling process enabling the public to apply for shares was completed with clarity and simplicity. Secondly, the assets being sold were under-valued which ensured that applicants, subjects to the terms of each offer, made profits. Thirdly was the issue of market liquidity which brought into the equation a respected City operator. Brian Winterflood had created Winterflood Securities, based in Dowgate Hill, EC4, who were market-makers, and added to the success of the privatisation programme.

Market-making worked as follows. A shareholder wants to sell some shares. There may be any one of a number of reasons. It can be simply to 'take profits'. Even having to pay capital gains tax still leaves surplus money assuming the sale price exceeds the purchase costs which, with privatisations, was usually the case. Perhaps a shareholder is finalising a personal divorce and needs to hand over a cash settlement. There are many reasons. The sale takes place by the shareholder having an account with a stockbroker who may well be holding the share certificate on behalf of the client. Instructions, usually by telephone, are given and the stockbroker will telephone a market-maker who, in the case of privatisations, will be, more often than not, Winterflood Securities. The dealer there will be told that the stock being 'dealt' (transacted) is 'X company';

at this point there is no mention of whether it is a 'buy' or 'sell' order. There will follow a 'buy' and 'sell' quote. If the client is selling shares the stockbroker will hear the 'buy' quote and accept it, or not. The 'buy' quote reflects the fact that the market-maker is buying the shares for their own account. They will hold the shares in the hopes of selling them on at a profit.

If the stockbroker's client has put an order limit on the deal wherein the stockbroker will have been instructed to sell shares at a limit of (say) 180p, if Winterflood quote a 'buy' price of 175p, the transaction will not be completed.

The stockbroker will return to his client who may agree to accept the lower amount.

The key point was that the market for privatisation shares was 'liquid': it was nearly always possible to complete a transaction. In the market for smaller company shares the risk of being unable to sell stock is always present (known as 'illiquidity') and investors become frustrated. The importance of the role undertaken by Winterflood Securities and its competitors in ensuring 'liquid' markets proved crucial to the eventual success of the concept of privatisation.

The staff at Basinghall Street settled down, driven by the common objective of encouraging wider share ownership. One day we noticed that Geoffrey Maddrell seemed deeply engrossed with a visitor: it was not long before Emma Kane joined the organisation. Over and above her remarkable talents she offered one significant advantage. Emma had been part of the Dewe Rogerson agency that had planned and promoted a number of the privatisation share issues and she knew the territory backwards. She had a little of the 'Thatcher' intensity about her and together we began to work for private investors but around the corner lay a much bigger prize.

Sir John Harvey-Jones and I, without knowing it, shared a common interest. 'The Guardian' newspaper described him as one of the best-known advocates of Transcendental Meditation (TM) which had been promoted by both the Beatles and the Beach Boys pop groups. In 1978, the founder (in the mid-1950s) of TM, the Indian born Maharishi Mahesh Yogi, purchased Mentmore Towers which was several miles outside Leighton Buzzard and set up the Maharishi Foundation. Teachers of TM began holding clinics locally and my doctor (and squash partner) decided to enrol and duly completed the course. I followed along later: we were taught to meditate in twenty-minute periods once or twice a day.

This was perfect for a London train commuter because Leighton Buzzard to Watford (halfway to Euston Station) was exactly twenty minutes in duration. One started by closing ones' eyes and relaxing for two minutes. Then you silently repeated the mantra (see below) at any pace that felt comfortable. On many occasions the conscious mind appeared to evaporate and I was flying around. Towards the end you stopped the exercise and waited for a further two minutes before opening your eyes.

The key was the mantra. The teacher, before the final lesson, explained that this was a word which the Maharishi had chosen specially for me. He asked me to give a solemn promise never to tell anybody my mantra, and I never have. The session became a bit mystic and there was a fragrance in the room. I was aware of a mouth whispering into my ear and I was given my mantra. Over the years I have used TM during periods of stress and found it to be effective. There are, of course, doubters particularly when the Maharishi suggested that TM could lead to world peace. My father, an accomplished pianist, said that for him playing Chopin's nocturnes gave him a similar experience.

The time has come to let Emma loose on the investment world of privatisations

The journey to Liverpool was arduous with road works causing delays on the M6 motorway but, after four hours, I arrived. Geoffrey Maddrell knew what I was hoping to achieve and had agreed to my proposal. I met a man and bought, for £6,000, the copyright of the term 'investment clubs'. The next day Geoffrey asked me to brief my colleagues in Basinghall Street. There was a discussion over the proposed name for the organisation. The agency engaged to make suggestions had come up with 'ProShare.' Everyone had an opinion except for Emma who said nothing. I completed my briefing on the possible way to encourage wider share ownership.

The next day she came into my office and stared at me. "The future is 'ProShare Investment Clubs'," she said. She was right. Over the next few years ProShare achieved much, including promoting employee share ownership schemes, but nothing compares to what happened over the following period. The faith shown by the sponsors was repaid in full as we turned Great Britain into a nation of investment clubs fulfilling the objective of wider share ownership. Throughout, Emma's passion and belief in the concept inspired the whole team.

I wrote a book on 'Investment Clubs' which was sponsored by Barclays Stockbrokers, a director of whom was Justin Urquhart Stewart, he of the red braces, who has gone on to be a popular financial commentator beloved by the media.

The ProShare team put together an investment club manual for use by investors wanting to set up a club and all that was needed was a campaign to promote the idea. Emma Kane went into overdrive.

The Secret of the Investment Club concept

The underlying reservation which dominates private investment is that of 'risk'. Individuals can, and do, lose money they can ill afford because they are chasing dreams of creating additional wealth often encouraged by unscrupulous sponsors. In today's modern financial environment, crowd-funding and crypto-currencies have led to substantial losses for optimistic investors.

The basic idea behind an investment club is that a

group of people, usually known to each other, agree to pool a regular (monthly) subscription which they can afford to lose – albeit that is not the objective. The aggregate amount is available for purchasing shares. Members bring to the meetings their ideas which are discussed and, if a majority are in agreement, an investment is made. There is usually a chairman and a finance officer who controls the funds and prepares a financial statement for each meeting. The ProShare Investment Manual provides all the paperwork including advice on taxation issues. A number of clubs founded in the mid-1980s are still running and lifelong friendships have been created.

The personal financial press adopted the concept and there were regular columns featuring clubs around the country. I visited many of them from Cornwall to Scotland. There was an active following in America and several European countries followed suit. ProShare Investment Clubs continues to operate (see www.proshareclubs.co.uk) but I made a decision to move on. Job done.

Emma, at a later stage, set up her own Public Relations Agency which developed into Redleaf Polhill before being sold to SEC Newgate UK where she is the chief executive. She was awarded the Freedom of the City of London in 2017.

Rushmere Wynne was growing slowly and I was pleased to return full time to my office above Knolls Squash Club. One day at lunchtime I played my Barclays bank manager, we then had a coffee together in the bar and he left to drive back into Leighton Buzzard. Neither of us would have imagined that an hour later I would be on the telephone to him.

The Most Extraordinary Decision I Ever Made

The original decision to relocate from Birmingham to Leighton Buzzard and our home in Redwood Glade was based, in part, to the proximity of Knolls Squash Club. This beautiful Grade II listed building was the head office of a timber importing company. The owner had added six squash courts and was building up a popular sports outlet. He then decided to lease out the club on a commercial basis and a member took it on. The atmosphere changed as the profit motive began to change the ethos of the club. The Rushmere Wynne offices were outside the lease agreement and I paid rent to the freeholder with whom I had a cordial relationship.

On the day that I had played squash at lunchtime with bank manager Stuart Ross, I went into the lounge and listened to the leaseholder sounding off about the brewery with whom he had fallen out and announcing that he was selling the lease. I went upstairs and spoke to the owner who said that he would welcome my proposed purchase and suggested we start again with a fresh agreement. He then made a mistake. I went into my office and telephoned the bank manager who expressed surprise at hearing from me. I asked him if he would agree to an overdraft of £30,000 to allow me to buy the lease of the club. He said that he would mark it up within the next hour and wished me well. Three days later I was the leasehold owner of Knolls Squash Club.

The mistake that the owner made was not apparent at the time. In the new lease he included an option to purchase the freehold for £300,000 which at that time seemed a rather full valuation. It was a struggle to turn the club into a paying proposition but three years later, together with a club member, Mick Compton, perhaps the best commercial partner I ever had, and in the light of surging property prices, we exercised the option to the fury of the owner who tried several dirty tricks to avoid the sale. It did not pay to mess around with Mick. Later we added thirteen bedrooms and turned 'The Knolls' into a hotel and country club. Then we received an offer from a local builder and 'The Knolls' became what it is today, a wonderful rest home for the elderly surrounded by majestic Redwood trees more usually found in California and China.

The five years I spent running the club remain a fulfilling memory. As with many things in life, a majority of the members were fabulous and appreciated our efforts to turn 'The Knolls' into a great club. A few were troublesome: that's life.

Friday nights were popular as members celebrated the end of the working week and, in particular, there was a group from a local village, Brickhill, who spent a lot of money at the bar. One week they called me over and told me that they had voted me the worst squash club owner ever. I replied by falling into their trap with the counter that I was the best operator in the country. Their leader spoke.

"Right, Tony Drury," he said, "if you're so clever get Jahangir Khan here for an exhibition match." Ouch.

By common consent, Pakistani-born Jahangir is the greatest squash player of all time. Now 59, he won the world open title six times and the British Open championships ten times from 1982 to 1991. I refereed him several times at Wembley. I made some enquiries and ascertained that his manager was the legendary football agent Mel Stein who represented Paul Gascoigne and Alan Shearer. I telephoned his office and, to my surprise, was transferred to him. I explained who I was.

"Tone," he said, and despite having never spoken to me he continued, "how are you? How's the family?"

I said that I wanted Jahangir Khan for an exhibition match and Mel said, "you've got him." I fell off my chair and struggled to reseat myself.

"£5,000," said Mel whereupon I descended to the floor for a second time. I explained that this was Leighton Buzzard and I could not afford his quotation. Mel said that there was no negotiation but I should say in touch which I did: I phoned him every month but to no avail. Then, early on a Monday morning, my phone rang: it was Mel. There had been a last-minute cancellation and I could have Jahangir in two days' time for £1,000. I sold the event to the club members in two hours.

The gallery overlooking the show squash court sat sixty people; we let in over eighty and broke health and safety regulations; nobody cared. I knew Neil Harvey, the British number one squash champion, and telephoned him to ask if he fancied playing Jahangir. He said, "I'm leaving now." He did play Jahangir and in a forty-minutes match he won two points.

What stayed with me most was that when I introduced Jahangir on to the show court the members simply exploded and the applause went on and on. He was a courteous and modest man who brought dignity to wherever he played the game of squash. The following Friday evening I went over to the group from Brickhill and served them with free drinks. Why not? Their challenge gave the club one of its greatest ever evenings.

The club had a strong first team led by David Peck who was nearing national top ten status. He was coached at a Thames Valley club by a New Zealander called Bryce Taylor who shot to fame when he introduced to the sport an unknown fellow countrywoman, Sue Devoy, who, from nowhere, in 1985, won the world title which she repeated three more times. She was awarded the MBE in 1986 and made a Dame in 1998. She returned to New Zealand to become a race relations commissioner, amongst several high-profile positions she occupied.

Back at 'The Knolls' we decided to organise a woman's championship at the club and attracted most of the world's top ten players. We added a fashion show; it was a great success. Sue Devoy played at a professional level well above most of the other entrants and won the prize of £500. As I handed her a cheque, she gave me a hug.

Some years later when back in London, I was told that we were employing a New Zealand-born secretary. I made myself known to her without attracting much interest. I asked her if she knew of Susan Devoy whereupon her face lit up and she explained that Sue was her personal inspiration. I hesitated but could not resist the temptation.

"Would it surprise you to know that Sue Devoy once gave me a hug?" I boasted. The secretary looked at me rather quizzically.

"I was giving her a cheque for £500 at the time," I explained. She stared at me.

"Yeah. Nah," she said, "I would want a cheque for £500 before hugging you."

*****

CHAPTER SIX
THE FORTUNES OF THE
HEADLINE MAKERS VARY RATHER
MARKEDLY

Mrs Thatcher departed from the prime minister's office in 1990 into retirement and thus began the torrid period of Conservative John Major's government which attracted damaging press negativity. Then, in November 1991, Robert Maxwell committed suicide by jumping off his yacht 'Lady Ghislaine' and the extent of his financial corruption became apparent.

One other personality succeeded in pushing them both aside. In December 1992, Diana, Princess of Wales, formally separated from Prince Charles and continued to be the darling of the press.

This brought in Bryce Taylor, who I knew both as mentor to my number one player at Knolls Squash Club and as the coach of Sue Devoy to whom I had given a cheque for £500. Bryce moved on and became the owner of LA Fitness Centre in Isleworth, west London. He wrote to Diana, Princess of Wales and invited her to use his gym. In the letter he sent were these words: 'We will do all we can to ensure your privacy.' The princess was to use the centre around one hundred times. Unbeknown to her, Bryce Taylor secretly took pictures of her in the gym which he sold to the 'Daily Mirror'.

In the outcry that followed he said that the princess wanted to be noticed. During a television interview he pleaded: "What was Princess Diana doing there in the first place if she didn't want to be seen?" At a later stage there was an apology and a financial settlement for damages including an amount paid to a charity chosen by the princess.

During the public outcry that followed the publishing

85

of the photographs, Bryce Taylor was invited by a German television channel to be interviewed and give his side of the story. The programme started with a discussion on the substantive issue of privacy and Taylor defended his actions with some vigour. He was then asked if his rationale over secrecy applied to himself which he accepted it was. Then the interviewer said that they were going to show a film taken in his hotel room the previous evening when he was watching a pornographic channel. Taylor fled from the studio and returned to New Zealand.

A family crisis takes centre stage

Emma, our daughter, was being bullied at school. It was something that took many weeks to materialise and Judy, together with the teachers, worked out that Emma could not clearly see the blackboard and the students were making fun of her: several took it further. That precipitated visits to the optician but, despite trying various prescriptions, nothing changed. This led to the involvement of the doctor and finally we ended up in Harley Street where Emma was examined by a consultant ophthalmologist. Mr Spalton spent a long time examining her eyes and then delivered the shattering diagnosis.

Emma was suffering from dominant optic atrophy which meant that the nerve taking the message from her eyes to her brain contained a genetic chink which resulted in a fuzzy picture. With medical advancements and the innovation of understanding DNA, modern treatment offers hope to the relatively few people who suffer from this complaint. For Emma there was no remedy and eventually her eyes deteriorated to such an extent that she relies full time on her guide dog. She qualified from Lancaster University and is having a successful career in education.

Several years later, the optician told Judy that she could not drive a car again. Her eyes have offered a limited hazy vision and she has weathered the condition with great fortitude. Our son Chris seemed to be free of the problem and became a professional golfer after winning the Bedfordshire Under 16s championship. He gained his Professional Golfers Association (PGA) qualification and was appointed the assistant professional at West Herts Golf Club, just outside Watford. Then he lost his driving licence and finally his sight deteriorated to such an extent he was unable to pass health and safety requirements as part of the coaching protocol. He turned back to being an amateur golfer and plays off a single figure handicap despite not being able to see his drive off the tee beyond one hundred yards, if that.

Big Bang, and we are not talking about Dodge City

There was one other seismic event which dominated the legacy of Mrs Thatcher's reign as prime minister although much of the overview centred on the Chancellor of the Exchequer, Nigel Lawson, and the successor Labour Chancellor Gordon Brown who faced a financial crisis during his term as prime minister (2007 to 2010). It was, however, Mrs Thatcher who negotiated a 1983 agreement between the Government and the London Stock Exchange (LSE) which settled a complex antitrust case which had been initiated by the Office of Fair Trading against the LSE. At its heart was the Restrictive Trade Practices Act 1956 which included fixed minimum commissions and the 'single capacity' rule. This enforced a separation between stockbrokers acting as agents for their clients on commission and stockjobbers who made the markets (known as market-makers) and provided liquidity by holding shares on their books. This was the role fulfilled by Winterflood Securities as described in Chapter Five.

Outside the City the changes initiated on 27 October 1986, dubbed 'Big Bang', when the LSE rules changed, were technical. The consequences were rather different. The London markets became much more transparent. There was a wave of takeovers and foreign competitors began to move into hitherto protected activities, often taking offices in East London's Canary Wharf.

'Big Bang' blew up the City of London. The term, as explained to the readers of the popular press financial pages, was about the deregulation of financial markets and, in 1986, was adopted to describe the abolition of fixed commission charges and to establish the definition of stockjobbers and stockbrokers on the LSE. The open outcry method of dealing (where stockjobbers shouted at each other when trying to negotiate transactions) changed into screen-based electronic trading. Share dealing was brought much more into the popular domain and opened up the markets for the Government's privatisation programme.

The political scene was experiencing change as the 'Iron Lady' reached the end of the parliamentary road and, in 1990, John Major, succeeding her as Prime Minister, began a struggle to contain internal party disagreements over the United Kingdom's membership of the European Union. I chaired a meeting of party members belonging to the Conservative constituency of South West Bedfordshire, in Dunstable, and I honestly feared that a fight might break out such was the polarised venom in the room.

John Major won the April 1992 General Election with 336 seats against Neil Kinnock's Labour total of 271 (an increase of 40 seats) and the Liberal Democrats' Paddy Ashdown who claimed 46 MPs. Five years later, in May 1997, the world changed as Tony Blair swept to power. Labour's 418 seats contrasted with the Conservative total of 165. Conservative Campaign Headquarters set up a unit to try to find jobs for members of parliament who were now unemployed. Three years later it had not placed all the names on its books.

By coincidence, the next speaker at the South West Bedfordshire Conservative's annual dinner was John Major. It was a few weeks after his electoral cataclysm. He delivered the most extraordinary political speech I had ever heard as he delved into how the Conservatives were the greatest ever political grouping known in modern social history. I recall that I was deputed to give the vote of thanks!

The new Conservative leader was the youthful William Hague who was badly advised. If he had waited, he might have become the prime minister the voters wanted as Blairism (and the government of Gordon Brown) wavered and lost its popular appeal. He lasted until 2001.

*

Having sold the building containing the Knolls Squash Club, I returned full time to the building of Rushmere Wynne as a financial publishing company helped by the growth in numbers of private investors. We moved to offices in Leighton Buzzard although I was continually travelling into London. At the heart of the success of London as a financial centre was the growth of the London Stock Exchange (LSE).

Originally a meeting in coffee shops of share agents it began to operate more formally in 1773 when it opened a dealing room and coffee shop in Sweeting's Alley on the north side of the river Thames, moving to Capel Court in 1802. In 1812, it introduced its first 'rules book' and a little over forty years later the innovative telegraph machine made prices from the New York trading floor available twenty minutes later, overtaken in the 1870s by the ticker tape innovation.

In 1914 the London Exchange played a key role in achieving the liquidation of twenty-five per cent of British overseas securities to finance the cost of the First World War. A new motto, 'My Word is My Bond' was introduced in 1923 and in the last year of the Second World War, a German V2 rocket made a direct hit on its building.

In 1970 the Market Price Display System showing seven hundred real time share prices came in and two years later the Exchange moved to 125, Old Broad Street where its tower had twenty-six floors. In conjunction with the 'Financial Times' in 1984, the

Financial Times Stock Exchange (FTSE) 100 index was launched followed by 'Big Bang' in 1986.
But a sensational enterprise was about to be introduced.

'If you aim higher than you expect, you could reach higher than you dreamed.'

Richard Branson's truism certainly applied to the planners at the London Stock Exchange who, in 1995, introduced what went on to become the most successful junior stock market in the world. The Alternative Investment Market (AIM) was designed for smaller quoted companies. It started with ten companies and at its peak had listed over 3,800. Entry regulations were less demanding although there was an innovative system of applicant companies needing both a Nomad (a Nominated Adviser) approved by the Exchange who was responsible for ensuring the rule book was followed and a Nominated Broker who controlled fund-raising and share-dealing. One company could fulfil both functions. The facility attracted considerable attention from foreign companies especially in the Far East. It was a spectacular success.

*

It seemed a good idea at the time

At Rushmere Wynne we were publishing more financial titles and building on the growth in the numbers of private shareholders. An explanation of 'charting' when 'experts' used pricing graphs to interpret trends in future price movements sold particularly well. Michael Walters, the deputy city editor of the 'Daily Mail', who had now written 'How to Make a Killing in AIM Shares' told me that charts tell you what the insider dealers already knew, perhaps a little cynically.

'Insider trading' is a criminal offence and occurs where

an individual or institution uses privileged information to make money by buying or selling shares before the market is informed of a particular development. The classical case is when one company intends to launch a bid to buy a rival and often at a price above the current market quotation. Although using that information to make profits (by buying the shares before the price rises when the 'bid' price is announced) is against the law, it is difficult to prove albeit the Financial Conduct Authority ('FCA'), the City regulator, has had some success in eradicating the practice.

Within Rushmere Wynne, and despite the popular financial press carrying stories from our books (the trick is to send the narrative to the City editors on a Monday morning when they are looking for copy for their upcoming columns), the frustration was that it was proving difficult to generate sales despite building relationships with the financial book shops. The later developments of social media, websites and Amazon sales would have been helpful.

I then received an introduction to the owners of another similar company and we joined forces and realised that the enlarged operation qualified under AIM rules: we applied for a share-trading facility raising substantial funds from investors. Then the worst of all worlds happened. My fellow director, the owner of the merged business, for reasons best known to her, started questioning everything I was trying to do and business came to a virtual halt. We had substantial funds in the bank but that was money the shareholders expected the directors to use to generate profits and pay out dividends. The AIM Nomad was suffering from high blood pressure and kept leaving meetings. Eventually the situation was such that the shares were suspended on the AIM; the troubled director left and I met a charismatic Welshman called Dr Colyn Gardner who had built Fairplace Training into a substantial and successful business. Shareholders agreed to a merger and the company name was changed to Birchin International whose shares were re-admitted to the AIM.

It became clear that Colyn wanted to run the whole company and so I resigned, perhaps not willingly but it was inevitable. I was treated fairly and received my contractual settlement. But I was once again out of employment.

My daughter Emma once said to me: "Your problem, Dad, is that you can't keep a job." I think she had a point.

The dawning of a dream come true

The next ten years working in the City proved to be the most satisfying period of my commercial career. I formed a corporate finance house which eventually became St Helen's Capital. We were regulated by what is now the Financial Conduct Authority (FCA) at a time when, because of concerns over market abuses (such as 'insider dealing'), regulation developed into a pivotal matter if you were working in the financial sector.

A market for smaller companies (OFEX) was developing with ambitions to rival the AIM. It later became PLUS Markets and was run by Simon Brickles, the former Head of AIM. We knew each other through the Rushmere Wynne period and he was supportive. It took a number of years to grow the company but when I departed in 2009, we had acted for over seventy companies and were thus the leading advisory firm.

I was now sixty-three years old and was travelling to places such as Singapore, Hong Kong and China and was being asked to be a director of various companies. This appealed as a final step before retiring and, when I left St Helen's Capital, I had seven directorships.

One of my board appointments was as chairman of a Hong Kong-based investment company which had listed its shares in London. In January 2001 I made my third visit to the Far East. I was already entranced by the architecture so reminiscent of the British Empire and on many occasions took the ferry from Kowloon City to Hong Kong Island. The 428 square miles are surrounded by the South China

Sea. It was then a territory of eight million people of whom a million were visible and seven million hidden away in relative poverty in high-rise blocks of flats. On one occasion I asked a taxi driver to take me to the backstreets but he refused my request.

Originally a mixture of farming and fishing villages, Hong Kong was ceded to the United Kingdom by the 1842 Treaty of Nanking. On 1 July 1997 it became Hong Kong SAR: the Hong Kong Special Administrative Region of the People's Republic of China. It is a global financial and commercial centre based on low taxation and free trade. It is home to the third-highest number of billionaires of any city in the world.

On this visit I was told that we were to cross the border in the north and enter Shenzhen, a vast Chinese metropolis famous for its shopping malls, skyscrapers and amusement parks. Five of us travelled by train to the border and approached immigration control. My four colleagues entered through a channel marked 'Chinese Passports' and I strolled towards another stating 'Foreign Passports'. I handed my documents to a rather surly police officer who placed my passport on his desk and turned it over page by page. Then, uttering aggressive sounds, he called another colleague who picked it up and also turned the pages.

Before I knew what was happening, a soldier armed with a shoulder rifle arrived, grabbed my arm and took me into a side room. I managed to make text contact with my colleagues but the connection was lost almost immediately.

The new location was about twenty feet square with a bench seat running around all four walls which were constructed of breeze block. There was a single light hanging from the ceiling and no windows. The centre contained a rickety wooden table and two chairs. The floor was covered in sawdust but not sufficiently to conceal some suspicious reddish stains. There was an empty bucket in the corner. The guard suggested I sat down – at least, that was my interpretation of his action in pointing his rifle towards me.

My morale took a downturn as, suddenly, the door opened and a plaintive young Chinese girl was pushed towards the bench by a fearsome female guard. The girl's dress was torn and she had blood coming out of her mouth. Within five minutes another officer arrived and the girl was led away.

Thirty-five minutes later a smartly dressed Chinese official came in and said, in perfect English, "Mr Drury, please come with me." I followed him into an office where he offered me a seat and a glass of water. "I am so sorry, Mr Drury, but we thought that you are an illegal entrant." He picked up my passport. "You have a new British passport and we have never seen one before." Put another way, the British Foreign Office had failed to inform the Chinese authorities that they had introduced a revolutionary revised design and my renewal application had generated one of the first to be issued.

I re-joined my colleagues and before long we were in the inevitable Chinese restaurant where a circular serving tray offered a range of varying dishes. Some, such as steamed dumplings or stir-fried noodles, were safe but when the dish contained things that were wriggling or when the eyes stared up at you it was particularly disconcerting

*

In the June 2001 General Election, Tony Blair inflicted another slaughtering of the Conservative Party by winning a second term with 412, against William Hague's 166. The Liberal Democrats under Charles Kennedy came away with 52 MPs.

At the same count I was elected as a Conservative Bedfordshire County Councillor although the more exciting event was the securing, after three re-counts, of a new candidate. Andrew Selous became MP for South West Bedfordshire and has held that position ever since with a vastly increased majority. He is now a respected parliamentarian.

William Hague departed as party leader to be replaced by a surprise choice. Iain Duncan Smith (known as IDS) had been the Member of Parliament for Chingford and Woodford Green since 1992 but almost immediately struggled to make an impact in the face of Tony Blair's dominance of the political airwaves. At the party conference he said, "Do not underestimate the determination of a quiet man," and a year later, "... the quiet man is here to stay and he's turning up the volume."

As constituency chairman I was becoming keen to endorse support for Andrew Selous and managed to gain the agreement of the Conservative Campaign Headquarters that, providing the audience was more than two hundred, we could have Iain Duncan Smith as our guest of honour at the annual dinner. We linked with two other local constituencies and held the event at the Sculptor Gallery in Woburn Abbey. It has never ceased to amaze me the excitement that the appearance of the party leader generates. My rather poor sense of humour must now be rather apparent to you, the long-suffering reader, but one of my throwaway lines was, "You could elect Mr Blobby" (the character made famous on Noel Edmund's House Party, first appearing in 1992) "as the party leader and Conservative members would go into raptures."

The atmosphere at the Conservative dinner as guests arrived was electric. At one point there was a circle of members and a young person opposite me shouted out, "Mr Drury. I'm so excited. When will Mr Duncan Smith be arriving?" There was just one problem in answering her question. She was standing next to Iain Duncan Smith who, unnoticed, had slipped into the lounge.

It was not long before Michael Howard was elected to succeed him, leaving IDS to pursue his Eurosceptic views.

*

While St Helen's Capital was building up, Colyn Gardner was making an excellent leader at Birchin International in which I still had a useful shareholding and, in early 2000, managed to sell a portion. With the proceeds we bought a holiday home in Aberdovey, Gwynedd on the west coast of Wales which is better known as Cardigan Bay. Built on the seafront, the three-storey house was called 'Swn-y-Don' which translates into 'The Sound of the Waves'. For the next few years, it became our second home. Judy's mother, being Welsh born, was delighted and as I was Birmingham-born-and-bred, Wales was a regular destination. King Edwards Five Ways Grammar School owned a Welsh farm and we made several visits as part of our geography studies.

Wales was changing. When Judy and I first went there for holidays it was not unusual when entering a local shop for the locals to switch to speaking Welsh.

Following a devolution referendum in September 1997, by a narrow majority, the Welsh people voted to establish an Assembly based in Cardiff. Known as the Senedd, the Welsh Parliament first sat on 12 May 1999. The sixty elected members occupy a single chamber government. Plaid Cymru, the Party of Wales, wants national independence.

In perhaps crude terms, Wales is a split country of north and south with many fields and sheep in between them. The countryside, the mountains and the valleys are some of the most beautiful in the world. The people themselves are proud of their history and culture. We valued our time in the seaside village as much as anything we have done.

It was in the front room of 'Swn-y-Don' that I began writing my first work of fiction. 'Megan's Game' was based on the legend of the Bells of Aberdovey which says that if a woman is walking the beach at night and hears the bells of a sunken village, she may find love. A publishing friend of mine says that most people believe that they have a book inside them and, in most cases, that is where it should stay. I was an avid reader of fiction and the title 'Megan's Game' was a tribute to one of my favourite authors, Gerald Seymour, now aged 81 and approaching the publication of his fortieth crime and espionage title. His first book, published in 1975, was called 'Harry's Game'.

Writing 'Megan's Game' took me into the, at times, complex world of fiction writing where many thousands of aspiring authors yearn to be published and spend sometimes large sums of their savings in chasing the publishing 'holy grail' urged on by some, at times, rather unscrupulous so-called literary agents. While the successful few, J K Rowling and Lee Child are two outstanding examples, earn personal fortunes, it is salutary to realise that ninety-five per cent of published authors earn less than £5,000 annually in royalties.

I was to discover much of this as I developed my writing and 'Megan's Game' was later to take me to Shepperton Film Studios and a meeting with a producer of four James Bond films.

Before I give the impression that I was on the way to becoming a best-selling author I should tell you of a letter I received from a lady in Tring. It read:

Dear Mr Drury,

I have just read your book and I must tell you that my six-year-old son writes better English than you.

Yours faithfully …

While there was a stable economic background in the early years of the twenty-first century, and Kylie Minogue and Britney Spears were high in the charts, the global world was becoming more violent. A new term entered the history books: '9/11', the eleventh of September 2001 when four co-ordinated suicide terrorist attacks, organised by al-

Qaeda, saw four hijacked planes crash into buildings including the Twin Towers of the World Trade Centre in New York and the Pentagon in Arlington County, Virginia. Over 3,000 people lost their lives. The War on Terror was launched. Tony Blair was vocal in his support of American foreign policy. I visited New York two months following the '9/11' attacks during a particularly hot spell. Although the restoration work had started, people were standing around bemused and, in several cases, were wiping their eyes.

The British prime minister maintained his support of American foreign policy into 2003 when 45,000 UK troops represented twenty-five per cent of the military force when America invaded Iraq on the basis of believing there were weapons of mass destruction hidden in underground bunkers. In October 2005 the President, Saddam Hussein, was tried for crimes against humanity and on 30 December 2006 executed by hanging.

Earlier in that same year, London was hit by the 7/7 suicide bombers' attacks when, at around 8.50am, three underground trains were blown up, killing thirty-nine people and injuring around seven hundred travellers. A further thirteen died when the upstairs deck of a bus was destroyed by bombs in Tavistock Square.

On the horizon there was another storm blowing up, this one of an economic nature, but with fearsome consequences.

*****

CHAPTER SEVEN
NO BILL, IT'S NOT MONICA, IT'S A CONFLAGRATION OF GLOBAL MARKETS

The global financial crisis of 2007-2008 seemed to pass by the forty-second president of the United States of America. In 1996 Bill Clinton began sexual relationships with a White House intern, Monica Lewinsky, and managed to keep it secret until 1998 when the story broke. He was impeached by the House of Representatives but was acquitted. He later became a supporter of the convicted fraudster Elizabeth Holmes as mentioned in Chapter Four. In April 2022 he was photographed on stage with Tony Blair at the Crypto Bahamas Conference which was co-organised by Sam Bankman-Fried's crypto derivative exchange FTX. Late in 2022, the company filed for Chapter 11 bankruptcy, Bankman-Fried was arrested in the Bahamas, extradited to the United States where he was charged with wire, commodities and securities fraud and money laundering. He denies all the charges.

The cause of the global financial collapse had originated two decades earlier when the US Congress passed legislation designed to encourage affordable housing. This led to the rapid growth of predatory financial products which were targeted at low-income, ill-informed house buyers, often members of racial minorities. The federal regulators never realised what was happening and the US Government was caught totally by surprise when the onset of the crisis began. The discovery of mortgage-backed securities tied to falling real estate values precipitated the mayhem until, finally, the bankruptcy of Lehman Brothers in September 2008 led to an international banking collapse. The American authorities tried everything to avert mass bail-outs of financial institutions which were engulfed by defaults and losses. Unemployment and suicides increased. In 2010 the Dodd-Frank Wall Street Reform and Consumer Protection Act was passed to promote the financial stability of the United States of America.

The global financial collapse coincided with the three years, 2007 to 2010, when Gordon Brown became the Labour prime minister after a bitter and messy battle with Tony Blair. As much as critics respected his time as chancellor of the exchequer when he tried hard to impose sanctions on Whitehall spending, as prime minister his uncertain temperament led him to struggle to maintain public support. Initially there was speculation that he would call a snap general election and Labour launched a rather strange 'Not Flash, Just Gordon' advertising campaign. He faced questions over political donations and lost a string of local elections as well as by-election defeats in Crewe and Glasgow. It was, however, the financial crisis that led to his coming election defeat.

The sub-prime mortgage crisis in the United States, as the British press referred to it, spread to the United Kingdom where there was a run on a British Bank. Northern Rock, which had allowed prudential standards of lending to fly out of the window, had to be rescued by twenty billion pounds of taxpayers' money. The Labour Chancellor of the Exchequer, Alistair Darling, faced daily pressures as the contagion spread. The economy was now in deep recession, unemployment took off and homes were being repossessed.

In the May 2010 General Election, David Cameron won 217 seats, Labour lost 87 but the Conservatives were 20 seats short of a majority in the House of Commons. The Conservatives and the Liberal Democrats entered into a coalition agreement and Cameron became prime minister.

How to play Chinese Chequers in a Beijing hospital

The markets were in retreat and I lost two more

directorships as the Chinese and Hong Kong companies could see no further value in retaining their London share trading facilities and thus did not need me. I decided to visit perhaps the best of the businesses I represented, an agricultural enterprise in Beijing, and prepared a revised business plan for the chairman to consider. Travelling in China is not easy although the hotels have caught up to western standards. I was determined to have a successful trip despite the global problems facing the world in 2008. The other challenge travelling in China posed was that, in my experience, some foreign-language Chinese speak pidgin English without any fluency. As one example, they could not say my name: 'Tony' became 'Pony'.

Although travelling in business class, the near-ten-hour flight from Heathrow to Beijing was a little testing partly because the individual next to me, by the time we were over the Ural Mountains, was drunk. I was met at the Beijing International Airport by the company chairman's PA, Frank Zhang.

"Ha!" he exclaimed on seeing me. "How ha hu, Pony?" We travelled the twenty-two kilometres to the hotel where we agreed that Frank would collect me the next morning.

"Sleep hell, Pony," he said as he returned to his car.

I was exhausted and so I booked in and went straight to my room where I raided the fridge and drank copious amounts of water. I sent a message home and dived underneath the bedclothes anticipating a welcome night's sleep.

Awaking early the next morning it was immediately clear something was wrong. The main clue was that the covering sheet was soaked in blood and I was scratching my left thigh. I leaped out of the bed and looked down. My upper leg was a mass of red, bleeding flakes of skin. There were times during my Chinese adventures that being over five thousand miles away from home was a rather solitary existence.

I showered but that seemed to irritate the infected area

and so I dressed and struggled down to reception whereupon Fang was waiting for me. She was dressed in a red outfit, perhaps five feet, one inch in height, dark-haired and Oriental-looking which was rather obvious except I was in no state to realise the obvious. Her name badge was in place. Fang in Mandarin means 'fragrance'.

"Whot hu hant?" she asked.

"I need to see a doctor," I pleaded.

"Wi?" she asked.

"I'm not very well," I diagnosed.

"Hat is hong wiv hu?" Fang pursued relentlessly, while a gathering of other guests around me was starting to demonstrate their impatience with my situation.

"I have a hash," I answered as the circumstances started to affect my composure.

"Hair is hash?" asked my inquisitor.

I looked around and considered pushing away the man behind me who was becoming aggressive but, having tasted a brief period of Chinese imprisonment, decided against it. I turned back and faced Fang.

"It's on my leg," I explained.

"I hont to see hit," demanded the hotel receptionist.

I am committed to trying to improve international relationships but the instruction that I must lower my trousers in the middle of a hotel in Beijing was testing my patriotism and so I left Fang and returned to my hotel room. I showered again and decided that the rash was even more angry whereupon there was a knock at my door. As I responded to the call, Frank Zhang appeared beaming with early morning energy. I invited him into my room.

"How har hu, Pony?" he asked.

I told Frank about my rash and asked whether he could arrange for me to see a doctor.

"Hi hont to see hash," announced Frank.

"Bugger this," I said to myself and dropped my trousers.

"Ho, hu ha hill," yelled Frank.

Events then moved rather quickly. Frank spoke to his chairman who instructed that he would send his car and the chauffeur would take me to the hospital for non-residents situated in the centre of Beijing. Frank was considerate and said little during the two-hour journey. We arrived and I was taken into reception where, to my utter relief, the staff spoke fluent English. I was offered a range of services, chose the appropriate option, paid the bill with my credit card and ended up in a treatment room, covered with a cotton robe and lying on a stretcher whereupon the doctor spoke to me.

"Hi fella, I'm Dr Hayward Derryman and I'm on secondment from California."

We struck up an immediate friendship as Hayward completed a full examination before staring at my rash.

If you are medically allergic to skin rashes, please don't read on

"Buddy," he pronounced, "you're in good condition but I have no idea what this skin problem is. I think it might be syphilis," whereupon my special relationship with Americans collapsed. The doctor disappeared and came back about ten minutes later.

"It's your lucky day," he said. "The consultant dermatologist is going to examine you in about half an hour."

I was taken to another part of the hospital and asked to sit down outside a room which had a notice saying 'Dr Wang'. Every few minutes a petite nurse came out and told me Dr Wang was almost ready to see me. Finally, I was instructed to enter whereupon Dr Wang stood up and invited me to sit down in front of her. I later realised that the dermatologist already knew what the diagnosis was going to be but she wanted a full resume of my health records and when I said that I rarely needed to see an English doctor she replied, "I consider it a privilege that I am able to treat you today."

TONY DRURY

I was asked to lie on the treatment table and Dr Wang examined my rash. She then instructed the nurse to return my gown and I was once again sitting in front of her. Dr Wang was in her mid-forties and professionally impressive.

"Mr Drury," she began, "you are suffering from psoriasis. We see many cases here often as a consequence of the perils of long international flights, dry air and stress. Have you been troubled by any particular tensions of late?" I wondered whether my encounter with Fang would count but I simply shook my head. "Dr Derryman," she continued, "has given you a good general health prognosis but your leg is one of the worst cases I have seen for some time. When you return home, you must see your own doctors immediately so that my diagnosis can be confirmed. Now, we will do all we can for you. We'll shower you using an antiseptic shampoo and then we will apply a cream which will need about an hour to be absorbed into your skin. I will also prescribe an antibiotic drug to counter any possible infection. I will see you before you leave."

Two nurses then led me to a separate room and guided me into a power-driven shower where a combination of soap bubbles, steam and their massaging of my skin made me wonder whether the amount I had paid on my credit card was rather a bargain. I found myself back on the treatment table where the senior of the two clinicians applied generous amounts of a cream covering the totality of my infected leg. An hour later, Dr Wang returned and used a dermatoscope to examine my skin. She pronounced herself happy with the improvement to my condition and said that she could now discharge me.

She handed me a tube of cream. "It is called Corticosteroid," she said, "but please confirm with your doctors that they agree with my diagnosis and treatment." Apart from my concern that I might breach medical ethics, my cream-covered leg suggested that my impulse to perhaps embrace the good doctor was misplaced. But, wow, was Dr Wang rather special?!

104

I was not well enough the next day to consider working and spent the time in bed albeit Frank Zhang called in three times. I did not tell Judy because there was no need to worry her. Things improved and I was able the next day to complete the schedule and spend useful time with the chairman who agreed to maintain their London share trading facility.

I returned to the United Kingdom and saw my doctor who said I was recovering well but who changed the prescription. When I was back in my Leighton Buzzard office, I told Irene, my long-suffering assistant, about the medical incident. She rolled up the sleeve of her blouse and covering her elbow was a horrible rash. "My doctor says it's eczema," she said. "It's in other places," she added and without any element of self-pity, she told me that she fights it every day of her life. I went on to the internet because I decided I wanted to know more about psoriasis:

Psoriasis is a skin condition causing flaky patches which form itchy or sore scales more often appearing on elbows, knees, scalp and the lower back. It affects around two people out of one hundred in the United Kingdom usually in adults between 20 and 30 years old and equally between men and women. It is a long-lasting (chronic) disease where symptoms can be periodic. Its cause is thought to be problems with the immune system in that the body's defence against disease and infection attacks healthy skin cells in error. Skin cells are made and replaced every three to four weeks. With patients suffering from psoriasis this process only takes between three to seven days. A 'trigger' is an event which can cause an outbreak including injuries to skin and throat infections.

During my brief consultation with Dr Wang in Beijing she tried to identify the 'trigger' which may have caused my outbreak: the demands of a long air flight, dry air and stress.

Cures for psoriasis are rare. Initially vitamin D analogues or corticosteroids will be tried together with various creams and ointments.

For more severe conditions phototherapy involving exposing the skin to certain types of ultraviolet light, may be tried. There can be psychological consequences as sufferers experience low self-esteem due to the effect on their appearance. For a few desperately unlucky people psoriasis can ruin their life. The Psoriasis Association offers advice and support.

Cameron takes over the world, help!

At the start of 2011, life was becoming decidedly challenging as I lost another directorship. Then, out of the blue, I received an offer for my shares in St Helen's Capital and I was able to tell Judy that I had paid off all the credit card debts I had accumulated. Politically I was empowered as David Cameron settled into being prime minister. Tony Blair disappeared, possibly into Africa, to make as much money as he could and Gordon Brown, cautious as always, went away to write his memoirs: 'My Life, Our Times', published in 2017, was well received and provided me with an entertaining and thoughtful autobiography of a complex politician.

Before taking office, David Cameron, in 1994, spent time at Carlton Communications as director of corporate affairs in a media company that in 1991 had won the ITV franchise for London Weekend Television. Cameron sat next to a pal of one of my contacts. I was told that his opinion of Cameron was that "all he wants is PM on his CV." That secured, he and his coalition partner Nick Clegg, agreed to the 2014 Scottish Independence Referendum, supported gay marriage and endorsed the UN-backed military action in Libya.

It was, however, economic austerity that was dominating the headlines and the work of the Chancellor of the Exchequer George Osborne proved outstanding. The ship was steadied, and his appointment in 2014 of Mark Carney as Governor of the Bank of England was well received in the Square Mile. The progress being made was reflected in the remarkable result of the May 2015 General

Election.

David Cameron increased the number of Conservative MPs to 330 (+24), Labour leader Ed Miliband lost 26 seats (down to 232) but the result that shook many people was Nick Clegg's Liberal Democrats, who, despite being in coalition, lost 49 seats leaving them with 8. To the north of the border the claymores were being sharpened as the Scottish National Party under Nicola Sturgeon put 56 elected representatives (+50) into Westminster.

"Ho, ho, ho," exclaimed the policeman. "You, Tony Drury, are coming with us."

Life in the Square Mile remained tough as austerity created uncertainty and fear. It also led some of us to perhaps take risks that, on reflection, were ill-advised. The fraudster at the centre of this tale was introduced to me by a well-respected corporate lawyer who later admitted he had made a misjudgement. The conman convinced me that he had surplus funds and was keen to finance my books and films. 'Travelling in hope' is not the best strategy but that's what I did until I pressed him to provide evidence of his goodwill. He gave me a cheque for ten thousand pounds which raised my morale until his bank declined to honour it. Of course, he had a plausible reason and told me to re-present the cheque but by now I had taken a telephone call from a police officer who was to become a friend and, to this day, entertains me with his detective anecdotes. This is how Detective Constable David Palmer of the Gwent Fraud Squad tells the story in his forthcoming autobiography:

And that year, I met Tony Drury. Tony worked in the finance industry and had some evidence for us regarding Mohammed Miah who'd tried and failed to obtain investment from or through Tony. We agreed to meet in a café near London Wall, so named because it represented the City limits at one time. Ty (Detective Constable Tyrone Broome) and I sat in the café and I saw a gentleman enter who I thought may be him. So, I rang him on my phone and thus confirmed it was him when he picked up the call. We took a statement from him and left our cards.

To this day I recall entering the coffee shop feeling rather apprehensive. I was quite experienced in meeting police officers because at one time I was chairman of Leighton Buzzard's Crime Prevention Panel and, as a Bedfordshire County Councillor, was called upon to meet local police to sort out constituency issues. This, however, was more demanding and when my phone rang, and I looked around, I spotted two Welsh giants who were staring at me. We connected and then David and Tyrone marched me down London Wall, walking either side of me, to my solicitor's office where they took my statement. I was able to support their eventual arrest (and subsequent conviction) of Mohammed Miah, because the 'bounced cheque' was a criminal offence.

David has pursued a career in publishing in the investigation, productivity and personal development fields and his book, 'Three Resolutions: How Understanding and Applying Three Simple Concepts Can Change and Recharge Your Life' captures the lessons and experiences of being in the front line of law enforcement.

The bank account becomes a work of fiction

In 2012, I was introduced to a person who remains a valued friend to this day.

Simon Petherick studied Modern History at Merton College, Oxford and entered publishing at Robert Hale in London before moving to Michael Joseph, publishers, writing copy for them. He founded his own publishing company Beautiful Books and built up to around one hundred titles and several excellent winners. However, austerity was making life difficult and he struggled to raise the capital base that publishing requires because you have to meet the cost of publishing books before you can sell them. He decided to sell the company and has moved on to apply his undoubted talents to other areas of literary work.

Before that happened, I was introduced to Simon and we discussed the possibility of taking on 'Megan's Game' but events overtook that event. Simon continues to advise (and criticise!) me to this day while he has forged an impressive career as an author and ghost-writer.

The development of Amazon books was opening up the self-publishing market and so I formed City Fiction and published 'Megan's Game' myself. Not long after I met Dave Lyons who was ahead of me in establishing Raven Crest Books. He agreed to join me as the publisher and remains a director of City Fiction to this day. We launched the title at a City venue and attracted a wide-ranging audience. 'City A.M.', the Square Mile financial newspaper, gave us an encouraging write-up. I visited Waterstones in Milton Keynes and they agreed to let me complete a book signing. In total I attended six of their branches including two bookshops in London and Leeds.

These occasions were always eventful. The strict ruling from Waterstones was that the author cannot directly approach potential buyers: one waits at the table displaying one's titles until someone shows an interest. I used to cheat a little and ask 'browsing' customers if they had found a book to interest them? On a Saturday morning in Milton Keynes, by 10.00am, I had sold three Victoria Hislop titles before I sold one of mine. On one occasion at the Waterstones outlet in Hemel Hempstead, after two hours I had not moved a single title. My response was to go outside and pay a woman to come in and buy my book! The visit to Leeds was memorable. An older person came up to my table immediately after the doors opened and I offered her a copy of my second DCI Sarah Rudd novels, 'The Deal'. She stared at me and then said, "The doctor says I have a year to live." Later, a rather dour Yorkshireman picked up a copy and asked me if it was set in Yorkshire. He did not give me time to answer his question. "If it's not staged in Yorkshire, you can shove it," he said. Waterstones then changed their policy and concentrated on 'celebrity' events and I was no longer wanted. Then I met Teresa!

I was at a Square Mile reception when I ran into a public relations operative who I had met briefly in the past. Teresa Quinlan was the founder of Love PR London. She had a sad story to tell in that her husband had died tragically and she was left to tidy up his business affairs and raise three sons. I suggested that I might support her commercial activities (and I did sort out a dispute with the VATman) in return for her PR support for my books; I was nearing publishing my second DCI Sarah Rudd (the police officer I had created) book, 'The Deal'.

Teresa telephoned me. What I did not know was that she had her offices at Shepperton Film Studios in west London and had shown 'Megan's Game' to her neighbour, Paul Tucker, a highly respected producer of four of the early James Bond films. She told me that he was interested in making 'Megan's Game' into a film. One of my shareholders in City Fiction, Michael MacDougall, who was my stockbroker based in Milton Keynes, offered to put up £100,000 in working capital. This initially paid for the script to be written, which brought in Crispian Sallis, an award-winning set designer and now writer, who prepared a brilliant version of my book. Heavens! All that I needed to do was to raise six million pounds to make the film. I once asked Paul Tucker, "Can you make a film for one million pounds?" He replied, "Yes, you can. Do you want anyone to watch it?"

There is much fraud and dishonesty in film financing as investors become starry-eyed at the thought of meeting the screen stars. It makes the raising of serious funding more challenging. I spent a year in London trying to generate the funds. This also meant our capital reserves were being used up at an increasingly rapid rate. I was to visit Shepperton Studios (now effectively partly taken over by Netflix) on many occasions and never lost the sense of history. Occasionally Paul Tucker used to meet me at the BAFTA Club in Piccadilly or the Groucho Club in Dean Street, Westminster. We've never given up but, as yet, we have not managed to make a film of 'Megan's Game'.

In November 2012 our grandson Henry James Drury joined us and became a fulfilling part of our lives. In October 2014 Judy and I moved to Bedford, renting a house for one year while we planned our future. Judy joined the Three Rivers Church, an evangelical base, and it has become an important part of her life. We are still in the house we moved into nine years ago and love it!

*****

CHAPTER EIGHT
INTO THE UNKNOWN: AND HOW!

It was early 2015 and I was sixty-eight years old. The Square Mile career was over and I was trying to become a successful author (in truth, I still am). Two years earlier I had listened to one of the greats speaking at a publishing conference. Sadly, he was a disgraced Conservative having been imprisoned from 2001 to 2003 for committing perjury and perverting the course of justice, but for many readers Jeffrey Archer remains one of the greatest ever fictional storytellers of modern popular literature. For me, 'Shall We Tell the President?', which is part of the Kane and Abel series, is my favourite Archer novel but there are many to read and enjoy. At this conference he said that every author believes their latest work is their best ever. I accept that reality, especially as during the writing and pre-publication period your optimism is high. Then your world begins to fall apart once, following launch day, the reviews start appearing.

A Square Mile anecdote might exemplify what can happen. When your title appears on Amazon Books you watch every day hoping a four-star, or even five-star, write-up will appear. Obviously, the author encourages family and friends to add their contributions but it is hard work. I have an associate, Simon Keiro-Watson, with whom I have worked with in the City and he is a great supporter of my books and has invested his savings into City Fiction. Following the publication of the fourth DCI Sarah Rudd detective series, I sent him a copy. To my frustration, no review appeared on Amazon. A gentle and polite reminder failed to generate a response. My frustration began to boil over and so I arranged to meet him in King William Street, near to Monument tube station. He was as cheerful as always. I bought him a coffee and made my pitch. "Simon," I began, "we have been friends for many years. I can't understand why you have not submitted your thoughts on my new novel?".

He stirred his coffee and smiled. "It's simple, Tony," he said. "I am a fan of your writing but I don't think 'A Flash of Lightning' is a particularly good read. It merits two-stars in my opinion but perhaps I can stretch it to three because the background of the Great Train Robbery was clever. I've not put up a review because I did not want to offend you."

There were mixed emotions on this occasion. As Jeffrey Archer had stated, I thought the latest DCI Sarah Rudd story was the best I had produced. Simon did not agree. We shook hands and I said I would leave it to him. At a later stage a three-star review appeared and was well written. Simon explained the weakness of the storyline and I realised that 'A Flash of Lightning' was not the best-seller I had imagined.

However, my argument, calling on Robert Louis Stevenson's philosophy, is that 'It is better to travel hopefully than to arrive.' The complete quote continues, 'And the true success is to labour'. Perhaps not written with his usual clarity but the meaning is clear. I'll press on as a writer. In my will I have stated that on my tombstone I want the epitaph, 'Have the sales improved?'

Judy settled well into Bedford and relished our trips south down the M1 motorway to Watford to be with our grandson Henry. His father, Chris, had overcome his eyesight setback and was building a new career for himself. Our daughter-in-law, Samantha, was a delight. Our daughter Emma lived in Bedford and was pursuing her career in education. I was still working with Teresa and going down to Shepperton Film Studios to meet with Paul Tucker. On two further occasions we thought that we had raised the funds to make the film of 'Megan's Game' but to no avail.

"Tony, we need you."

You would think that after several decades in the City I

would know all the signs but the words spoken by an associate, who ran a corporate advisory firm based in Queen Victoria Street, put me on my guard. But he did need me! His firm was acting for a

ese company that was listing its shares on the NEX Exchange Growth Market, the successor to PLUS Markets. Their application hung in the balance because the applications panel had turned down the proposed chairman and had allowed twenty-four hours for the advisor to find a suitable replacement. He had proposed me to the board of directors of the firm from Tokyo who had accepted his recommendation as had NEX Exchange – with two conditions.

The first was that I attend a meeting the next day in London with the directors of NEX Exchange which I did together with two of the company directors who had flown in that morning. The meeting lasted more than two hours and was demanding. Their second demand was interesting. They approved the application on condition I visited Japan within seven days and satisfied myself on the pedigree of the company. I was to be paid a decent salary.

On the train back to Bedford I asked myself what I knew about Japan? My first thought was a little bizarre. I have always been an avid reader of prisoner of war books and my favourite, which I had read many times, was called 'The Naked Island' by an Australian, Russell Braddon. In the Second World War, he had been imprisoned in Pudu gaol in Changi and then forced to be part of Force H which worked on building the Thai-Burma railway. He, unlike many of his compatriots, survived the brutality of his Japanese guards by trying to find humour even in the bleakest of circumstances. He accepted that in the Bushido moral code being a prisoner of war was a disgrace but he never forgave.

As the train sped through St Albans station, I remembered that in August 1945 the Americans dropped two atomic bombs, the first on Hiroshima and the second on Nagasaki, killing hundreds of thousands of Japanese people.

Four days later I began the journey by boarding a plane at Heathrow Airport and travelling six thousand miles, landing at Haneda International Airport and travelling the nine miles into the centre of Tokyo, where I was booked in to a five-star hotel. I was collected the next morning and taken to the offices which were in the technology heart of the capital. Within an hour I was chairing a board meeting with five fellow directors (two of whom I had met in London). My interpreter was Julia who was whispering in my ear all the time. After thirty minutes I realised that nobody had the vaguest idea what was happening so I called time out and went and sat in a lounge area. Julia joined me.

She was the daughter of an American father, who was now a professor of English at Tokyo University, and a Japanese mother; she had been born in Hawaii. She was twenty-two years old and I was to discover that she lived in fear of losing her job such was the unemployment situation in Japan. One evening, we had finished late and she insisted on coming with me back to the hotel. As I alighted from the taxi, I told her to go home and have a rest. "Oh no," she said, "I am going back to the office." She looked after me during my three visits to Japan but then left the company and secured a marketing position with Amazon.

We struggled on but the rest of the day proved frustrating and finally I called the board meeting to an end. I asked my fellow directors to be in attendance the following morning at nine o'clock. Then, suspecting what was the problem, I booked one of the offices and went in with Julia and her laptop. I dictated to her the minutes of the board meeting I was trying to hold. She was efficient and within two hours we had a final copy translated into Japanese which she delivered personally to all the directors.

The next morning the atmosphere was transformed as my colleagues bowed and stood up, laughed, smiled and started working. We had a direction of travel and they now understood what was happening. We went through about eight iterations of the minutes and finally we reached agreement which each director signed before the document was sent to London. We then did what Japanese always do: we had a meal in an elegant restaurant.

The company Ganapati Plc, named after Ganesh the Hindu god of prosperity and the remover of obstacles, was developing a branded product range for the iGaming market as well as software (Apps) for social media and consumer games. It employed several prize-winning designers and the creative artistry was breath-taking. It later obtained financial licences for its gaming products from Malta where I was to visit several times.

Following the start of the coronavirus pandemic in early 2020, travelling was curtailed and Ganapati was forced to close its British operations and return to Japan. I completed my term as chairman in June 2020 by ensuring the fidelity of its final market operations and the treatment of shareholders. I was left with some wonderful memories.

The first features I registered during the initial trip was the cleanliness of the islands and the cities I visited, no graffiti or street drunkenness, total (apparent) following of law and order and the politeness of the people. Everyone bowed to each other. The work ethic was phenomenal and my colleagues gave their all to the success of the company. I felt that I did not really gain their respect for about twelve months but following my second visit when we had to deal with several difficult market issues, one of which I solved single-handedly, the atmosphere changed and we ended up working well together. It was an extraordinary conclusion to my City career.

How much weight have you lost?

There was to be a further development to the Ganapati story. The corporate adviser who had introduced me to the company provided invaluable support throughout my time as chairman and we often used to meet for breakfast at the 'One Lombard' restaurant opposite Bank tube station by the Bank of England. When in town, Ganapati directors would join us. In January 2019 my associate appeared at our table and we immediately realised that he had lost about two or even three stone in weight. We were astounded and lavish in our admiration for his self-discipline.

He told a remarkable story: he had met a woman at a pre-Christmas cocktail party and somehow their conversation led to her revealing that she had a tattoo on her back. Quite how they reached that conclusion is not known but it was agreed that if he lost thirty-five pounds in weight, she'd show him her tattoo. Perhaps there had been several glasses of champagne consumed during their time together but it had triggered a reaction. He revised his diet, stopped drinking alcohol and every evening walked around Ealing Common for two hours listening to audio books through his headphones. He was on his way to achieving the target agreed.

I thought that as it was an unusual tale, perhaps I could write it up as a short story and, with his agreement, I did. 'The Forbidden Tattoo' was published in the autumn of 2019 on Amazon Books and is repeated in the final chapter of this autobiography. A few months after our breakfast together, I met my contact and was delighted to hear that he was maintaining the weight loss. I asked him if he had been shown her tattoo. "That would be telling," he laughed. "But she liked your story."

*

PLEASE, don't say that word under any circumstances

To break the tedium of reading about my career, here, dear reader, is a question for you. What is the most odious word in the English language? Before you ponder further here's another question. What could cause two mature men to fall out during a trip to Leicester? My friend Richard, my neighbour for over forty years in Redwood Glade, and I travelled together to watch his beloved Leicester Tigers play rugby. He was a calm and knowledgeable companion but if the referee gave a decision against the home side, he would metamorphose into an aggressive abuser of the official. On this particular trip to watch Tigers play Wasps (before their financial difficulties) we fell out on the outward journey two miles north of Milton Keynes and were hardly on speaking terms five hours later on arriving home. Because of one word. He was a 'remainer' and I was a 'leaver'. Not only did friends fall out, but so did families, work colleagues and politicians (many Scottish voters remain angry at the result). The word, of course, is BREXIT. David Cameron left his job.

The event, obviously a merger of 'British' and 'Exit', brought to a head the political schism which had dominated the Conservatives for many years. I have mentioned already possible fights amongst the members. It was brought to a head on 23 June 2016 when, in a UK Referendum, 51.8% of the voters wanted to leave. David Cameron resigned as Prime Minister almost immediately and shortly afterwards as a member of parliament. The Washington Post described him as having 'sped away without a backwards glance'.

In the argument between myself and Richard during our trip to see Leicester Tigers, my then neighbour, always passionate and thoughtful, seemed to lose his composure over the result. When I suggested it was the democratic process at work he answered, "What's that got to do with it? I must correct the result." He was not alone and due to the agonising and tedious Parliamentary process, it was not until 11.00pm on 31 January 2020 that the United Kingdom finally left the European Union, a member of which it had been since 1 January 1973. In January 2023 the Conservative government began the debate over the Procurement Bill which will 'rip up bureaucratic EU regulations'. The tensions caused by the Northern Ireland Protocol continued to fuel division amongst members of parliament although, in late February, the Conservative Prime Minister, Rishi Sunak, seemed to have negotiated a settlement. It was hoped that power sharing in Northern Ireland could be re-introduced.

In the City, European regulations had created a wave of new rules. The 2007 introduction of the 'Markets in Financial Instruments Directive' (MiFID) was intended to increase transparency across EU financial markets and to standardise regulatory disclosures for firms. In 2018 a second tranche labelled MiFID II came in and, although the UK was withdrawing from the EU, financial firms had to introduce the new rules. It led to a quasi-financial police force called compliance officers: every firm needed one or more.

A contact of mine at a competing corporate finance firm caused a stir by opening up an office in Belgium. He received a visit from his UK regulator, the Financial Conduct Authority (FCA), who asked to inspect his regulatory compliance records. His compliance officer produced a number of folders showing that the firm's legal advisers had properly ensured that all MiFID regulations were being met. The FCA official was unimpressed by that and reminded my contact that, EU rules or not, his firm was in the hands of the FCA and the Belgium office was not meeting with their standards. My contact closed it down. Behind his back we applauded the FCA because some of us doubted the competence and integrity of the Belgium proposal. FCA rules rule (poor English, but you get the point); EU rules come second.

*

In early 2022, I was completing my daily walk around Bedford Park as part of the brigade of elderly health adherents trying desperately to keep fit and so avoid the need to see the doctor (not that any appointments were readily available) when I came to a decision: I gave up politics, emotionally. It is the only positive thing that Boris Johnson has ever done for me. I was unable to accept any further his, in my opinion and judgement, abuse of power and lack of social morality.

Politics had been a large part of my life as chairman of South West Bedfordshire Conservatives, as a County Councillor, as leader of the Blue (Welsh) Dragons in London and for the last ten years as a member of the Thursday night political forum on Three Counties Radio with the charismatic Roberto Perrone. I was, on occasions, asked to take part in the JVS morning show, because he liked me being rude about Boris.

The Conservatives had been in power for twelve years since 2010 mainly because Labour could not unveil another Tony Blair. David Cameron (2010 – 2016) promised much but delivered a Brexit exit, much to his own surprise. Theresa May (2016 -2019), despite her personal integrity, simply had no empathy and could not relate to people unless they were giving her large cheques – as her post-office earnings of around two and a half million pounds rather indicated. After she was ousted by her fellow MPs, in came Boris Johnson (2019 -2022) who saw himself as a reincarnated Winston Churchill. Whilst hugely intelligent and learned, Johnson had no genuine social integrity. To him politics was an Etonian ball game where he used his personal appeal with voters to be elected regardless of the party manifesto, which he ignored. The UK had Johnson. America had Donald Trump. They were both ousted, Trump by American voters (despite his claim otherwise) and Johnson by Conservative MPs. I had 'left' by this point but the fifty days of Liz Truss as a hapless prime minister defied rational explanation.

In January 2023, SKY News, in conjunction with Tortoise Media, broadcast a series of 'revelations' called 'The Westminster Accounts' in which the outside earnings of members of parliament were detailed. The Prime Minister Rishi Sunak said, "What's the fuss? It's all published information." The initial SKY findings were based on 600,000 separate financial statements.

Everybody knows that the 'Westminster Gravy Train' is an insult to the hard-working British people, not helped by a privileged and disinterested monarchy and a House of Lords comprising around 780 sitting members making it the second largest assembly in the world (the biggest being the National Assembly of the Republic of China). The House of Lords contributes little to British society and with too many members milking their peerages for personal gain. During the coronavirus pandemic what did the House of Lords contribute to the national emergency? It has a constitutional role and its vetting of parliamentary draft bills formulated in the House of Commons is important. Perhaps an elected upper house of 200 members is more appropriate.

In 2020 Sir Keir Starmer, the Labour leader, asked the former prime minister Gordon Brown to consider 'the future of the union and the devolving of power, wealth and opportunity throughout the nation'. A commission was established including Labour councillors, MPs, Peers, legal experts and academics. Their report, published in December 2022, set out forty recommendations for constitutional change covering rights, devolution and reform to the House of Lords. It may well happen but perhaps I won't see it.

*

What a novel idea: no, it's a novella!

My writing career took a change of direction in unusual circumstances. One Sunday I went to the local newsagents for the papers when I noticed they were selling off old DVDs. I spotted the 1961 film 'Breakfast at Tiffany's', bought it and spent the afternoon watching it, twice. It was hard not to be transfixed by Audrey Hepburn's mesmeric performance as Holly Golightly and her guitar playing and singing of 'Moon River' on the fire escape outside her Manhattan flat remains this collector's prize memory. I researched the film and discovered it was based on a novella written by Truman Capote. The literary vehicle was new to me and my investigations led me to conclude that most were published by Penguin Modern Classics and the prizes available stipulated between 7,500 and 40,000 words. The word 'novella' originates from the Italian for 'novel'. Another characteristic is that a novella has limited punctuation with no chapter headings and no breaks apart from where the author needs to show a scene change.

Famous novellas include 'Of Mice and Men' by John Steinbeck (1937), 'Animal Farm' by George Orwell (1945) and 'Rita Hayworth and Shawshank Redemption' by Stephen King (1982), while 'On Chesil Beach' by Ian McEwan was made into a film in 2018 starring Saoirse Ronan.

I decided to write a modern-day novella based on 'Breakfast at Tiffany's' which became 'Lunch With Harry'. My friend Teresa loved the idea and created the Novella Nostalgia series where titles were inspired by iconic films. A solicitor pal, Oliver Richbell, helped me write 'Twelve Troubled Jurors' based on the Henry Fonda film '12 Angry Men' before producing his own brilliant creation 'Gloriana' inspired by the film 'Valkyrie'. My colleagues in City Fiction, Candy Denman and Billie-Jean Sandiford, produced their own works and R M Cartmel – a retired doctor and serial author – wrote 'Sabre Tooth' inspired by 'The Day of the Jackal'.

There was one more amazing adventure ahead. I was shopping in a supermarket and, on the bottom shelf of their entertainments section, I discovered a DVD of the 1947 film 'Gentleman's Agreement' starring Gregory Peck. I watched it three times before deciding my next move. It told the story of antisemitism in post-Second World War America. I have worked in the City with many Jews and have had a Jewish business partner for many years. I am a non-practising Christian. Judy is a member of Three Rivers Evangelical Church in Bedford. I was about to discover that I knew little about Judaism.

Finally, 'A Search for the Truth' was published telling the story of a university undergraduate Lily Jane who, to gain an honours degree, must write a dissertation titled 'To Define a Jew'. The initial research took over three months as I delved into the beauty and compelling (if, at times, tragic) history of the Jews. The novella was published and well received including positive reviews by several academic Jewish scholars and the office of the Archbishop of Canterbury. A suggestion arose that it could be turned into a film and I visited a friend in Jerusalem including spending their Sabbath walking around the holiest city in the world.

Antisemitism remains global and brings heartache to many wonderful people. A better understanding of Judaism might help change attitudes.

Of course, Robert Maxwell was a Jew – but that's life!

I spend much time trying to generate the necessary finance to make the film.

*****

CHAPTER NINE
A GLOBAL PANDEMIC DEVASTATES
THE UNITED KINGDOM

In 2012, during a visit to China when visiting a Beijing suburb where a factory belonging to one of my clients was situated, I became detached from my colleagues and found myself walking along trading streets. If you have been to Hong Kong and accessed the late-night markets where residents sleep in paper boxes piled on top of each other, nothing will surprise you. This was not night life; it was intimidating daytime reality with shops and trading frontages occupied by some fearsome-looking individuals some of whom were holding knives and other implements which they brandished or put into the pockets of their blood-stained overalls. It was busy, crowded, baffling and with pungent odours and poor (by Western standards) hygiene standards. I was alone for nearly three hours before I was located by one of my fellow directors who rushed me away from the area. It has been suggested that the COVID-19 pandemic which was to cause untold misery in the United Kingdom originated as a zoonotic (transferred from animal to human) disease originating in a seafood wholesale wet market in China. I do not doubt that hypothesis.

On 31 December 2019, the World Health Organisation (WHO) received information concerning the reported increasing numbers of cases of pneumonia in Wuhan City, in the Hubei Province of China. The cause was as suggested above. On 9 January 2020, the WHO announced that from samples taken from patients a new coronavirus had been identified. In February 2020 the virus was named as SARS-CoV-2 and the disease caused by it was identified as COVID-19. On 11 March the WHO declared that the COVID-19 outbreak was a global pandemic and stated that this was because of the rapid spread and severity of cases around the world.

It is premature to attempt to summarise the full consequences of COVID-19 on the Square Mile but financial markets are remarkably resilient and some operators made bucket-loads of money from the consequences of the pandemic, not always through legitimate operations.

'Stay Home. Protect the NHS. Save Lives'

On 19 March 2020, the Prime Minister proposed, "… we can turn the tide [of the coronavirus] within the next twelve weeks." Four days later the 'Stay at home' message was broadcast and on 26 March, 'The Health Protection (Coronavirus Restrictions) (England) Regulations 2020 were published. In February 2021, a four-step plan to ease restrictions was announced and in May the final steps to freedom were taken by government officials.

Every life (and new birth) across the four home countries was affected and the resurgence in early 2023 in China of new COVID-19 infections is a clear indication that the consequences of the pandemic are to remain in some form for years ahead.

The National Health Service (NHS) was launched in the United Kingdom by the Health Minister Aneurin Bevan who was part of Clement Atlee's Labour Government, on 5 July 1948. Devolution has created separate country arrangements but in England it remains the only publicly funded health system, paid for by taxation, in the whole world. The NHS is the second largest employer in Europe with 1.2 million equivalent full-time employees.

Politicians of all sides in the House of Commons keep 'reforming' the NHS and the Conservative Health Minister, Andrew Lansley, following the publication on 12 July 2010 of a White Paper titled 'Equity and Excellence, Liberating the NHS', introduced changes which some commentators believe are a significant part of the problems the NHS are facing today. In 2015, the health minister was elevated to the House of Lords.

Partly as a result of political meddling and latterly and more significantly the huge demands placed on it, particularly in the social care sector, as a result of COVID-19, the NHS is devolving into a two-tier system as more people resort to private health care services. In January 2023 a survey from the Office for National Statistics showed that 13% of adults had paid for private medical care in the previous twelve months. The City love it as they advise (for large fees) American equity funds who are using their wealth to buy up the various private doctor and hospital companies that are emerging, often created by entrepreneurial British-trained medical practitioners. It is now difficult to access NHS dentists; mine, a private surgery build by an enterprising Indian couple, was, in 2021, bought by BUPA and – of course – the fees have increased.

Occasionally the obvious is understated. There is a growing population in the UK: in 2022 it was 67.5 million people. In 2011, the figure was 63.2 million. There are additional challenges as, and despite the Brexit promises, the UK's rather porous borders are seeing refugees and illegal immigrants pouring through together with legitimate entrants from Hong Kong, Afghanistan and other places where the humanitarian side to the British character dominates.

A second factor affecting the NHS is revealed in the life expectancy tables published by Government. Currently, males from the most deprived areas will live, on average, to 73.5 which rises to 83.2 for those from the least-deprived areas. Females can expect to survive until they are 78.3 if from the most-deprived areas and 86.3 if residing in the least-deprived areas. Medically, and rather obviously, it is more demanding to care for people in their eighties than, as in previous decades, in their seventies. The latest Government figures show that in 2020 there were 15,200 citizens aged over one hundred years old. Judy says that women live longer because they work harder.

The Square Mile loves social trends and pays its analysts generous salaries to put their employer ahead of the crowd. An example is in the retail sector where City short-sellers made profits from realising that COVID-19 restrictions were going to wreck city-centre shopping malls and this is exactly what happened. A short-seller is an investor who sells a share (using a special financial instrument) in the belief they will be able to buy it back at a lower price. Other funds realised that the home delivery market was going to expand and invested in the growing numbers of enterprising companies occupying this developing space.

Since COVID-19 restrictions were introduced in March 2020, I have not travelled into London by train saving four hours a day or, seeing it from another standpoint, increasing my effective work time by four hours. The current 'work from home' conundrums are testing employer and union approaches to pay and conditions. In March 2022, I was seventy-five years old, retired from politics and I had accepted that it was time to age gracefully and walk round Bedford Park with the keep-fit brigade. But there was a new adventure coming.

Creative Support, social care and a new trainee support worker

The leaflet which was delivered though our letter box arrived on a day when I was feeling restless and not yet ready to join, full-time, the geriatric troopers. It was colourful and featured a rainbow heart with the words 'creative support' overlaid on top. It was inviting me to an open day with the question: 'Are you a warm, proactive person who is keen to make a difference?' and it continued 'We are hiring now: full, part-time, waking night and relief roles.' I read on:

Creative Support is a charitable social care provider with over 30 years' experience of providing person-centred care for people with a wide range of support needs. We are hiring compassionate people who can motivate and support individuals with a learning disability to enjoy a great quality of life in a supported living service in Bedford. Experience is not essential as you will be given full training and support.

I went along to their regional office in Bedford Business Centre and lit a fuse to an extraordinary four months. The people I met were unbelievably welcoming and committed and before I knew what was happening, I was completing an application form to apply to become a part-time support worker. James, the boss, masterminded the administration but it was not too long before I met Claire, the manager of Poplar Tree Court residential centre, which was a little more than a mile from where we lived.

The recruitment process was rigorous and initially included a long, testing afternoon where James and Claire wanted to understand exactly what I was all about – including role playing and situation analysis.

They contacted me and said that I was provisionally approved but then the Creative Support head office took over requesting a full CV, proof of eligibility to work in the UK, passport, an NHS Covid pass and an Enhanced Criminal Record Check Certificate. I also needed two referees which provoked a certain amount of humour as one of my referees said he had replied that I should not be supporting in a care home, I should be admitted into it.

How many modules?

Finally, on the first of August I began work at Poplar Tree Court working from 2.30pm to 10.00pm four days on, then one day off, two days on and so on. It worked out to one weekend in two. The building was owned by a housing association. There were eighteen well-furnished apartments situated in a pleasant residential area of Bedford, of which sixteen were occupied by service users funded by the local council and benefits.

I decided there were three separate challenges: to gain the confidence of James and Claire; to achieve acceptance by the other carers; and, to build relationships with the residents. Initially I was completely thrown by the training programme which involved forty-three eLearning modules. It could take up to two hours to master a module and, at the end of each session, there was a test which one had to pass before moving on to the next topic. These included, for example, 'The golden thread of Equality, Diversity and Human Rights' and 'How to work in a person-centred way' as well as 'Anti-Racism' and 'Infection Control'.

There were several hurdles but Claire guided me over them and eventually the training was completed albeit all staff members were required to maintain a continuing and 'testing' eLearning programme. This allowed me to concentrate on the staffroom. The 7.00am shift were responsible for checking all those present and attending to their basic needs, the care of their apartments, medical and shopping lists. The 2.30pm shift took over during a hand-over period and at 10.00pm one carer would stay on for the 'sleep-over' until 7.00am the following morning. There were strict COVID-19 hygiene protocols one of which, and often my job, was to wipe down the building's doors, handles and exit bars with an antiseptic wipe. I found I was quite good at balancing the service users' cash boxes which was completed twice a day.

The hub was the staffroom albeit Claire, in her office opposite, never missed a trick. There was a round table where we gathered; the door was nearly always open to enable service users to come in. One reason was that if they were leaving the premises, we needed to know that to ensure we could meet health and safety regulations including fire drills. At the heart of the activities was the working relationship between the carers because there were few days when they did not face challenges and time after time their ability to think out solutions was paramount.

Every service user was an individual, each with their own requirements, physical and mental conditions; a number were autistic, many with learning difficulties. The cooperation lay both inside Poplar Tree Court and outside with the various agencies, the council and the doctors. Some residents went out to social centres and gyms, others stayed in their rooms, a number used the communal lounge. Relatives came and went.

Each service user had a file and, at Claire's suggestion, I studied these becoming almost baffled by the degree of analysis which the writer had given the exercise. There were set targets and part of the work of the carers was to help service users achieve these. Each also had a day book where every action was recorded, the importance being that at any time, a fresh carer might need to know the position with an individual who needed assistance. Medications were given four times a day and were closely monitored. On the round table in the staffroom there was a 'communications book' which was used for that purpose. Claire would leave important messages therein although she also used text messages to reach us. There was a monthly staff meeting where sometimes James, but always Claire, formalised the reporting procedures.

After I had overcome the training challenges, I began to settle into being a trainee support worker. Women could look after women and men but generally men looked after men. There were birthday parties and occasional Friday night take-away meals. The process of assimilation was easier than I had anticipated because I quickly built up an incredible respect for the carers. They faced challenges all day long and their overwhelming desire to make a difference to the lives of service users was breath-taking. Most were on minimum wage payments.

One Saturday which will stay with me for a long time, was when there were just three of us on duty, two women and me. It was one situation after another. The fire alarms went off when a meal being heated in a microwave ignited, a lady fell over and we had to follow the strict protocols on assisting her and ensuring her welfare together with reporting the incident. Some service users liked us to cook their meals and I had four bookings at 5.00pm, 5.30pm, 6.00pm and 6.30pm. The individuals placed an importance on my reliability and punctuality and I sweated to ensure I keep to my timings until I reached my 6.00pm appointment. The man, highly intelligent and a bit playful, was standing by his door as I arrived at 6.00pm knowing that the 6.30pm service user would be waiting and I had thirty minutes to complete this assignment. He wanted baked potatoes and a salad together with cold chicken. No problem, I thought. That was until, for some unaccountable reason, the microwave was not working to full power and the potatoes remained stubbornly underdone. 6.30pm was approaching, the moaning was increasing in volume and so I informed my 'friend' that I was switching on the oven to finish heating the potatoes and his meal would be ready at 7.10pm. I sensed war was about to be declared, so I added, "And if you don't like it, I am going to throw your bloody dinner out of the window." I arrived back at 7.10pm to find that he was as good as gold and thanked me for looking after him. I wrote it up in the day book and confessed all. I was told off for my 'threat', quite fairly.

In October 2022, I threw in the towel. I understood the priority of meeting the needs of the service users but I felt a continuing pressure to perform, often in difficult circumstances. I still miss Poplar Tree Court, the carers and service users, and at Christmas I sent the staffroom a large Christmas cake and a letter thanking them for all they had taught me about social care. I received a text message: 'All the staff at PTC want to say a big thank you for the cake.'

Over the years both as an individual and as a politician I have had much to say about our medical services and, at a time when the public's faith in the NHS is wavering, it is easy to join the doubters. The four months at Poplar Tree

Court working with the most unbelievably dedicated carers taught me more than any other experience I have had. Deep in the heart of the system is something very decent and humane and I was privileged to be allowed a glance at it.

Interest free credit for the needy: that sounds an interesting concept

Having been brought up in a post-Second World War Methodist household, made to go to church three times on a Sunday (morning service, afternoon Sunday school and evening worship) and had religion taught to me at some length at school, it is perhaps not surprising that I am a non-practising Christian. I did not realise that was the correct label until I began researching for the novella 'A Search for the Truth' (as described in Chapter Eight) and trying to understand Judaism. I was often asked, mainly by Jews, "What is your religion?" Judy is a member of the Three Rivers Church, an evangelical church in Bedford, and her religion is very important to her. The pastor is Paul Sands, very Irish (Ulster-bred), very passionate, very honest and at the head of an important service to the community. An occasional morning coffee with Paul is an engagement I relish.

Religion, unexpectedly, was to come back into my life because I came across a remarkable Muslim called Saqhib Ali, a chartered accountant. He was promoting his business on LinkedIn and trying to attract non-executive directors. Eighteen months ago, I met him, became chairman of his company ZeroPA, and we have a coffee together every Saturday morning as well as regular board meetings. In recent times his commercial success has accelerated and helped me overcome the disappointment of leaving Creative Support and Poplar Tree Court.

In researching Judaism, I began to understand Islam and travelled to Jerusalem, a holy city for Judaism, Christianity and Islam. I visited the Temple Mount housing the Dome of the Rock which is recognised by all three religions as the site of Abraham's sacrifice. The Wailing (Western) Wall is famous worldwide and because of access restrictions is the nearest Jews can reach their holy centre. The Temple Mount is characterised by its gold-plated roof and is an Islamic shrine known as the Al-Aqsa compound.

Muslims adhere to Islam, meaning in Arabic 'submission to God'; it is a monotheistic religion which has the Quran, the foundation religious text of Islam, accepted as the verbatim word of the God of Abraham (Allah) as was revealed to the prophet Muhammad. In 2020 it was estimated that around 25% of the world's population are Muslim.

This must sound like an extract from Wikipedia, which, in truth, it is, but as my friendship with Saqhib matured I wanted to understand better the devout adherence to his religion. In building up the corporate governance of ZeroPA (a responsibility of the chairman) I was astounded by the quality of the people he was attracting: it is possibly one of the most talented board of directors I have ever chaired.

The mission of ZeroPA is to provide interest-free credit for the needy on a commercial basis. There are many competitors but they nearly always mislead their customers by applying hidden charges and other ruses. It is a 'fin-tech disrupter' which, in City terms, means it uses technology to operate a competitive business by challenging traditional providers.

The word 'disrupter' refers to the business model that seeks to use computer technology to disrupt the more established businesses by dramatically reducing the cost base.

There are three elements to the business model:

- the altruistic concept of providing interest free credit to those who are unable to access normal channels of finance by peer-to-peer charitable investors. This is

133

achieved by asking affluent individuals to provide interest-free money, taking the risk that they may not be repaid.

- ZeroPA facilitates the transaction but ensures that the funds go, not to the individual, but to the destination of the funds such as a white-goods supplier; the supplier pays ZeroPA a commission.

- ZeroPA assists the customer to manage funds better and plan their financial future; it will also introduce the customer to mainstream banking thereby earning an introductory referral fee.

Saqhib's hyperactive approach led to an introduction to the authorities on the Isle of Man and the registration of The Interest Free Loans Company Limited through the Department for Enterprise, Isle of Man.

The company has now succeeded in obtaining a Moneylenders Act 1991 Certificate of Registration. This has allowed a test period to begin the results of which will provide a clear indication of the commercial competence of the ZeroPA approach.

During my career in the City, I came across a variety of approaches to the making of money, including fighting off a number of dishonest operators. An interesting aspect to ZeroPA is that it is attracting seriously gifted people who are socially aware and want to be part of an organisation that can play a part in helping those most needing support in a responsible way. The credit for this goes to Saqhib Ali, a remarkable person.

An interesting aspect to ZeroPA is its valuation. In recent years, markets have followed the extraordinary wealth generated by Silicon Valley start-ups maximising internet and computer power. Fin-tech companies have achieved stella valuations as investors try to back the next Amazon, Google, Facebook, or Twitter. The latest investment into ZeroPA was completed at a valuation of £2 million. One day I asked Saqhib if ZeroPA had any direct competitors. He said that ZeroPA was unique and I confirm that statement having studied the marketplace and spoken to my fellow directors. Where does that leave ZeroPA? Watch this space!

Thus, reaching seventy-five years of age, I experienced a brief but rewarding experience with Creative Support at Poplar Tree Court and found myself chairing an innovative 'fin-tech disrupter' with social aspirations and created by a talented entrepreneur.

There has been one further development in the latter stages of my career which I will explain in the following chapter of this autobiography. There is time, however, for me to ask you, the reader, to consider the following question:

<u>Based on an informal survey I have conducted, what, generally, do older people conclude are the three most important ingredients necessary to achieve a happy and successful life?</u>

Please, before reading on, conceal yourself in a dark room or leave for a five-mile walk to enable you to reach your own conclusions. Then write them down on a piece of paper or record your thoughts on your mobile phone.

In pursuing the various answers to this challenge several subscribers suggested 'the ability to communicate'. This reminds me of a story some years ago when a good social friend admitted to me that he had been involved with a girlfriend and, in a fit of guilt, confessed all to his wife and suggested they went to consult a marriage counsellor.

Memories flood back of the sit-com series 'Men Behaving Badly' which ran from 1992 to 2014. The appalling Gary (Martin Clunes) and Tony (Neil Morrisey) spent their lives – when not drinking to excess – either, in Gary's case, arguing with Dorothy (Caroline Quintin) or, in Tony's daily toils, lustfully chasing the gorgeous Debs (Leslie Ash). The situation was reached where Dorothy (a nurse) persuaded Gary that they should go and consult with a relationship counsellor who was based at the hospital where she worked to discuss their troubles. Gary reluctantly relented and then spent the whole session trying to chat up the rather attractive counsellor. Slapstick comedy, most definitely, but nevertheless humorous.

My pal reported back that he had found the session constructive in that he realised he had been remiss in his lack of communication with his wife. She was in full agreement. On their arrival home she told him that she was going to implement the advice received during the meeting in that she would speak to him honestly. "I'm leaving you," she said, and did.

Interpersonal communications are decidedly relevant to the achieving of a fulfilling life but did not make the top three in my survey. Incidentally, there were a total of thirteen suggestions from my responders. In no particular order, the top three ingredients were:

- Sexual fulfilment
- Sufficient wealth (money)
- The correct body weight

Mention has been made of attitudes to sex when discussing, in Chapter Four, E L James's book, 'Fifty Shades of Grey', and the ambiguity of Megan's behaviour. My survey asked for headline answers only and one assumes that the participants who gave this answer were implying matrimonial/partnership fulfilment.

The second answer is self-evident and it is recognised that financial stresses are a key factor in marital/relationship breakdowns. The theme of wealth creation, making money honestly and/or corruptly, and not being able to pay one's bills, has been a consistent topic in the various chapters of this journey through the Square Mile.

The third, 'the correct body weight', needs some explanation. It is a subject which has occupied the last three years of my life. It began with Boris Johnson, I had an idea, and then I met Sarah, met again with Linda, went to Lincoln and had coffee with Toby, reconnected with Kathryn and, as always, shared the idea with Teresa. We all came together to pool our various professional skills in trying to devise a way to help people lose weight and live a healthier lifestyle. The next story in my autobiography follows.

*****

CHAPTER TEN
'IF WE CAN SORT OUT THE NATIONAL OBESITY CRISIS, WE CAN SORT OUT THE NHS'

(GB News: January 2023)

A business connection, apart from supporting Arsenal Football Club, was usually preoccupied by his health and a battle with type 2 diabetes. He was due to attend surgery for a monthly weigh-in but was late because he had refused to exit the bathroom until he had completed a bowel movement which he said was worth a pound off the reading. When he reached the doctors he immediately argued with the practice nurse because he insisted on taking off all his clothes before she weighed him. They compromised with him keeping on his boxer shorts and then, as he stood on the scales, they could not agree on the actual reading. He then accused the staff of using faulty equipment. Eventually an increase in weight was agreed and my associate was told that he must see a doctor. He waited forty minutes to meet with a locum who gave him a prescription to reduce his stress level.

A person's weight is, for many, a daily fixation: after waking up and checking for messages on their mobile phone and reading overnight emails, they enter the bathroom and weigh themselves. For many it is a matter of healthy living and staying within a weight range as part of a plan. Others fear of being overweight and the possible medical complications it might mean and continue to battle against adding additional pounds. Some see it as a matter of personal pride and self-respect. Unlucky weight watchers may be affected by medical conditions. A concern over the scales can lead to anorexia nervosa, an eating disorder where an individual may threaten their health by reducing significantly the amount they eat. There are possible psychological consequences when a loss of confidence, perhaps self-esteem, is caused by a failed period of attempted dieting.

There are many commercial opportunities generated by the passion to lose weight, ranging from the doctor's 'guaranteed to lose weight' diet best-selling book, to slimming clubs and gymnasiums where exercise is said to help the process. The more affluent members of society might employ a personal trainer who creates a disciplined environment by encouraging daily exercises and physical activity.

The medical world offers bariatric surgery involving gastric bands, gastric bypasses or sleeve gastrectomies wherein the stomach's capacity is reduced. Less than 6,000 such operations a year are undertaken by the NHS and usually for patients with a BMI (see below) of over 40. An increasing number of patients are flying to European medical centres for these operations. The actual national statistics for overweight and obesity (a BMI over 30 – please see below) are as follows in a report published in 'The Health Survey for England, 2021':

25.9% of adults in England are obese and a further 37.9% are overweight but not obese. Obesity is usually defined as having a body mass index (BMI) of 30 or above. A BMI between 25 and 30 is classified as 'overweight'.

The survey, published in December 2022, found that men are more likely than women to be overweight or obese (68.6% men, 59.0% women). People aged 45 – 74 are most likely to be overweight or obese. Since 1993, the proportion of adults in England who are overweight or obese has risen from 52.9% to 64.3%, and the proportion who are obese has risen from 14.9% to 28.0%. In the most deprived areas in England, the prevalence of being overweight or obese is nine percentage points higher than in the least deprived regions.

In October 2022, the World Health Organisation (WHO) stated that:

More than one billion people worldwide are obese – 650 million adults, 340 million adolescents and 39 million children. This number is still increasing. The WHO estimates that by 2025 approximately 167 million people – adults and children – will become less healthy because they are overweight or obese.

Overweight and obesity are measured by the BMI calculation: body mass index. Generally, it is accepted that a BMI over 30 is obese. It is calculated by dividing an individual's weight measured in kilograms by the square of their height measured in metres.

Is there a solution to the overweight/obesity conundrum?

There are around 28,000 full time GPs in the UK and thus there are 28,000 different opinions on how to lose weight. By common consent, dieting is the reducing of one's calorific intake and maximising the benefits of one's BMR – the basal metabolic rate – which is the speed that the body uses up the heat (energy) generated by the calories taken into the body.

If it was only that simple! The tables say that the percentage of adults in England who are overweight and/or obese is 64.3% Some doctors are overweight and a number are obese. A Royal College of Physicians report published in January 2023 estimated that around 700,000 people working in the NHS were overweight and/or obese.

The GB News item quoted at the start of this chapter suggesting that finding a solution to the overweight/obesity challenge might 'save the NHS', at a point in time when its future is under intense public and political scrutiny, offers a profound and simple logic. Many people are ill or are in hospital because they are either overweight or obese. If there is a way to help people reduce their weight and regain a healthy lifestyle, some of the pressures on the medical resources will be eased.

Yes, there is a possible solution to the overweight/obese challenge.

In April 2020, the Prime Minister was admitted to hospital suffering from COVID-19. It later emerged that he was around five feet nine inches tall and weighed a little over seventeen stone which gave him a BMI of around 35. After he recovered, he became focused on the issue of obesity and, until other matters assumed a greater importance (the war in Ukraine as one example), he publicised the medical concerns of the problem in the UK.

At this time, I was writing a regular column for a lively website – mrandmrs50plus – which aimed to support people moving into their retirement years. I was Mr Moan, self-opinionated and rude. I decided to ask the question: how would I encourage people to lose weight? The general consensus (subject to many provisos) is that, as explained above, it is a matter of consuming less calories (which generate the energy to run the body's organs) and keeping fit to maximise one's BMR which is the pace of consumption of the calorific intake.

I started by recognising that the vast majority of people know exactly how to lose weight. Their difficulty in doing so is that they cannot resist eating food often with a propensity for consuming carbohydrates. They eat a sensible, balanced meal and then are overcome by a desire for chips, pastries, biscuits or sweets. Often, as soon as they break their self-imposed diet, their self-discipline collapses and they decide to start another diet in a week's time.

The key to helping people lose weight was therefore to find a way of supporting them during the key moments when, if they are to adhere to an agreed diet, they must resist the temptation to consume what the slimming clubs call 'sins'. It is not so much the actual additional intake of calories that is the crucial matter. It is the psychological setback the individual experiences by 'giving in' to a perceived weakness.

My solution was to pay the dieter £100 for every pound in weight shed in a programme agreed with the GP and monitored by the clinical nurse.

My article, 'Obesity and Diabetes – Tony's Monday Moan,' was published later in the year and, unusually, generated interest from the website's readers. I therefore sent it to the Department of Health and Social Care who, a few weeks later, replied expressing their interest. They suggested I contact my local Clinical Commissioning Group (CCG, now replaced by larger Integrated Care Groups).

I met Dr Sarah Whiteman, a highly regarded GP and the medical director of the Bedfordshire, Luton and Milton Keynes CCG, who expressed interest in the idea of offering financial incentives to enable people to beat the hunger pangs. I introduced Sarah to Professor Linda Duffy of Middlesex University who had a wide-ranging knowledge of the psychology of dieting. I contacted Kathryn Bullock, a successful marketing entrepreneur with whom I had worked in London.

Then I travelled to Lincoln to discuss the matter with Toby Stephenson who ran my publishing website. He turned out to be socially aware and gave his time free to several medical charities. Finally, I discussed the proposal (as below) with Teresa who was working for two diabetes charities and had a wide-ranging knowledge of the issues involved. We were six in total and agreed to work together by forming a Community Interest Company called Earn Your Health (see www.earnyourhealth.org).

I wrote the foundation document, 'The Healthy Future Programme' (shown below), which we signed off and launched on 26 April 2021. We made steady progress until the COVID-19 restrictions and the pressures being faced by GPs and the NHS in general brought us to a halt. The six founders remain united in their determination to generate interest in the concept of offering financial incentives to encourage people to lose weight and improve their healthy lifestyles.

Here is the full text of the original 'Healthy Future Programme':

Earn Your Health Community Interest Company Limited is dedicated to helping overweight and obese people in the UK to benefit from The Healthy Future Programme. This Programme aims to lead to weight loss and a healthier lifestyle, by adopting a holistic approach.

The Healthy Future Programme

The available evidence suggests that millions of people find it difficult, if not impossible, to lose weight: it is that single barrier that must be overcome.

The solution, 'The Healthy Future Programme', aims to take place in the GP surgery or clinic. It's designed to ensure that patients diagnosed as being clinically overweight or obese receive guidance and are incentivised to help them face the battles ahead.

The goal is to help put the patient on the road to a healthy lifestyle enabling them to regain a healthy weight, whilst countering the consequences of excess weight and/or obesity.

The Healthy Future Programme works as follows:

Patient A visits their GP who recognises that they are overweight or obese. In the past the doctor has tried to help this patient by offering advice and dietary guidance but the patient fails to lose weight.

Patient A weighs twelve stone, two pounds and with the GP, they agree between them a target weight of nine stone is achievable and desirable, a loss of forty-four pounds. The doctor suggests enrolling the patient to join

'The Healthy Future Programme' and provides literature in the form of an explanatory brochure and a series of handouts explaining the prevalence of excess weight, obesity and dietary guidelines.

If in agreement of the concept Patient A consents to joining The Healthy Future Programme. On joining their weight is recorded at the Surgery by a Health Care Professional (HCP) who agrees regular check-ups and weigh-ins on a fortnightly basis.

On Patient A's first return appointment a weight loss of two pounds is recorded. The HCP will discuss with Patient A and assess how they are responding to the Programme. If everything is in order Patient A receives a payment of £200 (£100 for each pound in weight lost) paid by the surgery directly to the patient's bank account.

The Healthy Future Programme solution to excess weight and obesity is based on the incentive of receiving regular payments for achieving and maintaining weight loss.

This is the scale of payments to Patient A.

Agreed starting weight: Twelve stone, two pounds
Target: Nine stone.

- Loss of first fourteen pounds to reduce to eleven stone, two pounds: £1,400
- Achievement payment (for losing a stone/fourteen pounds): £500
- Loss of fourteen pounds to reduce to ten stone, two pounds: £1,400
- Achievement payment (for losing a second stone/fourteen pounds): £500
- Loss of fourteen pounds to reduce to nine stone, two pounds: £1,400

144

- Achievement payment (for losing a third stone/fourteen pounds): £500
- Loss of final two pounds to achieve target weight: £200
- 'The Healthy Future Gold Medal' payment for achieving the target: £1,000

Total payments: £6,900

Every six months thereafter Patient A returns to the surgery and is weighed. If the weight has stayed within three pounds of the original target, Patient A will receive a stability payment of **£500**. This will continue every six months for the next three years, a further total payment of **£3,000**.

A key to the success of the concept is the involvement of staff at the GP Surgery. Staff are further incentivised to motivate patients and are awarded cash bonuses. For example, when a patient reaches a first target of losing fourteen pounds, the staff share a bonus of **£1,000** (and again for the second and third fourteen pounds losses) and when a patient reaches an agreed target, the surgery receives **£5,000**.

In the example given above, when Patient A achieves the target of nine stone, the surgery will have received a total of **£8,000**. The staff themselves will be eligible to join the scheme. To control the additional administrative workload, it is proposed that, initially, each doctor within a practice can accept ten patients into the scheme.

The total outlay for Patient A achieving the agreed weight loss: **£17,900.**

Are the financial incentives subject to taxation?

This proposal contains a recommendation that Her Majesty's Revenue and Customs ("HMRC") are asked by the Department of Health and Social Care to give an exemption to the financial incentives from personal taxation assessment.

How much will the scheme cost?

It is only possible to provide an estimation because there are two variables —number of patients and weight lost.

In the example given above, a GP's Surgery where four doctors place ten patients each on the scheme (forty in all) and those patients individually lose forty-four pounds, the costs are, over (say) four years, as follows:

- Financial incentives paid to patient to achieve the target weight (as above): £6,900
- Payments (over three years) for staying within three pounds of the agreed weight: £3,000
- Payment to surgery staff 3 x £1,000 for weight loss: £3,000
- Payment to surgery for achieving overall target: £5,000

Total potential payment per patient: £17,900
Total payments from the surgery budget (40 x £17,900 over (say) four years): **£716,000**
Cost per year: £179,000

Initial financial summary

For an annual investment of £179,000, forty patients can be incentivised to achieve a target weight which the doctors believe is in their best interests. The figure quoted is probably a maximum as many patients will either need to lose less than the forty-four pounds used in the example above or not actually achieve the full target loss. A few may lose more than the forty-four pounds but they are likely to be exceptions to the general target range. Some will not manage to lose any weight. It is one of the hardest challenges any human being can face.

What is the total cost?

There are around 7,000 GP surgeries in England with an average of 8,000 patients registered. If one third of practices over time decide to introduce The Healthy Future Programme, the total potential cost is:

- 2,300 practices x £716,000 over four years: £1,646,800,000
- Cost per year: £411,700,000
- Total number of patients achieving weight loss targets: 92,000
- Cost per patient (over four years): £17,900
- Cost per patient (each year): £4,475

Who pays for the scheme?

There are three possibilities:

The Clinical Commissioning Groups (CCGs)

This is unlikely as most CCGs face huge pressures funding the current demands being made on them.

The National Health Service

This is the obvious source. Since 2013, local government have become responsible for improving the health of their population supported by the public health grant and specialist public health teams. However, the coronavirus pandemic caused the tearing up of the rule book. There is an obesity crisis. Perhaps it's time for the government to step in again.

Charities

The coronavirus crisis demonstrated the general public's huge respect and admiration for NHS staff and their dedication to help their patients. It is quite conceivable that a charity can be established to raise the funds to enable the scheme to be introduced.

What are the risks of fraud?

The proposal is a low-risk exercise but there may be some individuals who see an opportunity to make easy money:

The Patients – there will be a few individuals who will use ingenious methods to defraud the scheme. That will be a price worth paying because it is the benefits which accrue to the vast majority of patients, who want to lose weight fairly, that matters.

The Surgeries – the personal integrity of medical staff is very high but there may be a few who see an opportunity to make money. One control is to appoint NHS inspectors who have the power to make unannounced visits to GP practices to inspect their records. If there is any suspicion that the scheme is being misused the whole practice will be debarred from ever taking part again. The patients who may be legitimately on the scheme will have their contracts ended but offered another GP's practice to resume their weight-loss efforts.

What are the medical benefits of the proposed scheme?

Many, if not most, overweight and obese individuals yearn to lose weight. They will have tried the many and innovative ideas marketed to them. They may well have taken up their doctor's time in trying to understand the issues and perhaps changed their dietary habits. Some, if not many, will have already required surgical help to counter the various consequences of being obese.

To the patient who uses the scheme and loses weight, a whole new world awaits them. There is the self-respect engendered by feeling heathier, by standing on the scales and not being scared to look at the reading, the joy of wearing clothes that were too tight.

For many the additional funds will enable making healthier food choices when shopping or the chance to reward themselves with new clothes or a day out for the family. It's also proven than weight loss empowers people of all ages to become more physically active so the money could be used towards purchasing gym kits or joining a health club.

One of the greatest emotions in the world is to feel comfortable and attractive. The individual radiates self-confidence and self-respect. Their choice of clothing will be more appropriate and reflect their personalities rather than hide the bulges: bring back the bright colours!

To the surgery
It is essential that staff are fully invested and committed to the scheme as a team. The decision to partake will invariably be taken by the senior partner who will want to ensure that all their colleagues are on side. Overlooked by GPs, practice manager(s), receptionists, and nurses will be involved from the start as their patients start to lose weight.

To the NHS
The Healthy Future Programme will improve public health outcomes and reduce the demand for hospitalisation and outpatient appointments. There should be less complications, such as type 2 diabetes developing as a result of excess weight and obesity.

It is estimated that The Healthy Future Programme can save the NHS over £620 million!

The Department of Health Policy Paper states that, 'it is estimated that overweight and obesity related conditions across the UK are costing the NHS £6.1 billion each year.' The data is taken from a paper published in 'The Journal of Public Health Advance Access' dated 11 May 2011 which set out NHS costs in 2006 – 2007. The figure for 'Overweight and Obesity' is given as £5,146,000,000 and assumed therefore to be updated to £6.1 billion.

An article in the 'Daily Mail' (8 July 2020), '3 million are so fat they qualify for stomach ops', uses a study in the journal 'Obesity Surgery' which calculates that 7.3 per cent of England's adult population qualify for bariatric operations.

The procedures are costed at between £4,000 and £15,000. If the three million stated to be in need of surgery received treatment it could cost the NHS up to £45 billion. The study suggests that currently the NHS are providing 6,500 bariatric operations annually.

Using this latest study as a guide to calculating the possible economic benefits of 'The Healthy Future Programme' the qualification for bariatric surgery is based on adults with a BMI of 40+ and 30+ for those patients suffering from type 2 diabetes.

It is calculated that each doctor's list contains 1,960 adults who are obese. If, over time, 2,000 surgeries (out of 7,000) invoke 'The Healthy Future Programme' and five per cent of their obese patients (98) reduce their weight to below a BMI of 30 thereby avoiding bariatric surgery and/or type 2 diabetes, the potential saving to the NHS is 2,000 surgeries x 98 - 196,000 adults now under a BMI of 30. Assuming an average weight loss of two stone (twenty-eight pounds) the cost of the financial incentives is 196, £5,800 = £1.76 billion.

The cost saving to the NHS is £620 million.

The Proposed NHS Reform

In February 2021 the Secretary of State for Health and Social Care, the Right Honourable Matt Hancock MP announced proposed changes to the NHS. These include structural reforms to introduce integrated care systems, with the objective of bringing together different parts of the health system to work together to plan future patient care. NHS bodies will have a duty to collaborate. Patients will get more rights to choose private providers for NHS care.

The funding of the NHS is to be reformed.

*

Mr Angry, Mr Moan, Mr Nice Guy? Perhaps

If I am to be completely honest, I suspect that I have always had a little of the rebel in me. In politics that goes without saying because no party manifesto (even if, as is unlikely, the leaders keep to it when elected into government) can cater for all opinions. In my youth one was either right, a capitalist, a Conservative; or left, a supporter of the unions, with a belief in public ownership of assets and a Labour voter. Somewhere in between were the Liberals who wavered between left and right.

My religious stance of being a non-practicing Christian undoubtedly reflects my parents' insistence that I attend church three times on a Sunday which bred into me a resistance to the ministry. They were coming out of a desperate Second World War experience and the letdown that the years following meant with austerity, unemployment, a continuation of rationing and political change as Clement Atlee's Labour government went on a nationalisation spree while at the same time accepting American loans to prop up the Government's finances.

Added to this was the growing fear of Soviet invasion of western Europe and, at school, we played a game in history lessons guessing how long it would take the Russians to reach the French coast. I recall coming third with my calculation of four days.

My parents offset this demoralising social period with their Methodist worship and the communion of faith that John Wesley had inspired, their love of Charles Wesley hymns and the freedom to mix with fellow believers which held together their morale. On 2 June 1953, Queen Elizabeth II was crowned at Westminster Abbey and slowly a new dawn began to shine. There was one house in our road with a television set and we took turns to watch the ceremonial occasion. At school we were given tins of Cadbury chocolates and a mug featuring Her Majesty. I recall my mother spending the day shedding tears of joy.

Judy's grandfather was a Church of England minister and her mother was brought up in a vicarage with several servants. She gravitated to family worship attending on Christmas Day and certain festivals. For her, the move to Bedford and the joy of being part of the Three Rivers Evangelical Church was rejuvenating. I have enjoyed watching her preparing to lead the weekly bible class where a passage of scripture would be discussed.

My discovery of Judaism as a consequence of writing 'A Search for the Truth' was rewarding. When I visited Jerusalem in 2001 my host arranged for me to attend Friday night worship at a local synagogue at the start of their Sabbath. It was a privilege I'll never forget. There were about eighty men because the women appeared later in an upstairs gallery in their finery. I was given an order of service (reading, of course, from right to left) and the cantor sang with gusto and musical joy. Every so often someone would stand up, come over to where I was sitting, and shake my hand. I cannot understand antisemitism. It makes no sense to me.

My battle with authority started with Mercantile Credit

where I quickly built up a resentment of the public-school-educated board of directors. Later, as my own commercial activities developed I switched my aggression to the privileged minority (including the bloated monarchy) whilst staying a Conservative because small government, low taxation and enterprise to create wealth which could be distributed fairly, seemed reasonable. As I rose in the ranks, I had lunch many times at the Carlton Club in Westminster and met Members of Parliament at the House of Commons.

But I could never resist writing controversial material including a period of time when I was Mr Angry who expressed his views on a website called 'Enterprise Britain'. I progressed to Mr Moan on the mrandmrs50plus website as discussed above.

Then came the final decision to call a day on politics and certainly Boris Johnson's lack (to me) of personal integrity and Liz Truss's fifty days as prime minister caused a certain frustration. I have moved into retirement keeping my views to myself. Along has come ZeroPA, and 'Earn Your Health' and so the future, whatever that means, will be interesting. Mr Nice Guy? A little unlikely!

* * *

CHAPTER ELEVEN
HOW MANY MARKS WILL YOU
AWARD ME FOR THE WRITING OF
THIS AUTOBIOGRAPHY?

In the 1976 film 'The Eagle Has Landed', from the fictional war book by Jack Higgins, directed by John Sturges and starring Michael Caine (now 89), Admiral Canaris, head of the German Abwehr (counter-intelligence) is ordered by Adolf Hitler to make a feasibility study to capture the British Prime Minister, Winston Churchill. He orders staff officer Oberst Radl to undertake the exercise. At the same time, Radl receives an intelligence report from a sleeper agent in England informing the Abwehr that Churchill is to visit a Norfolk village.

He asks his subordinate if he has studied the works of the Swiss psychoanalyst, Carl Jung, who he describes as a great man. He explains that Jung's theory of synchronicity might be appropriate in the preparation of the plan to capture Churchill. The proposal that two unrelated events can come together to produce an outcome.

This chapter is based on the theory of synchronicity. The two events which have come together to produce the reassurance I am seeking, that I have met the mandate set me in writing this autobiography by relating my personal stories to the social, financial and political backgrounds at the time they took place, are as follows:

Event One:

During the coronavirus lockdown we went many months (in fact, a year and a half) without being able to visit Watford and be with our grandson, Henry. After a time, telephone calls and zoom sessions began to pale and so I started sending Henry periodic quizzes. My envelope to him would contain perhaps fifteen or even twenty questions, often illustrated (name this island?), a sealed envelope with the answers and a second labelled 'Henry's Prize' containing a £10 note.

Amazingly, Henry always answered all the questions and won the prize. The Christmas alphabet quiz, in December 2022, was based on twenty-six questions where each answer began with a sequential letter of the alphabet, A – Z. Henry's envelope arrived in early January 2023 due to the post office strikes!

Event Two:

The inspiration behind this book is Simon Petherick who encouraged me to finish its chapters. His guidance was clear: the various stages of my career in the City should reflect the social, political and financial backgrounds, avoiding the temptation to become consumed by personal matters. The research and delving into the archives have occupied an absorbing period during the cold winter months (the full impact of climate change has not yet reached Bedford although last summer was rather warm with two days in excess of forty degrees centigrade).

The end is nearing but I am left with the conundrum of whether I have met Simon's dictate. But Jung's help is to hand: synchronicity, whereby event one and event two come together to generate an interesting conclusion to this autobiography (I hope!).

I have set out below a quiz for you, dear reader, comprising twenty questions. If you have read the various chapters and absorbed the social, political and financial backgrounds, as mandated by Simon, then you should be able to answer all twenty questions. The correct solutions are shown below. No £10 note, I'm afraid, but my undying admiration for reaching this far.

Have fun!

The Square Mile Tales Quiz

There are twenty questions coming and you may be able to answer all of them correctly.

Question One
Name the English cleric who founded the independent Methodist movement.

Question Two
In which English county is the carpet town of Kidderminster situated?

Question Three
Who played Private Pike in the BBC's comedy series 'Dad's Army' which ran from 1968 to 1977?

Question Four
In which year did the Secondary Banking Crisis start?

Question Five
On 5 November 1991, Robert Maxwell committed suicide off the Canary Islands by jumping from his yacht into the sea water. What was the name of the boat?

Question Six
Many people consider that Jahangir Khan (now 59) is the greatest squash player of all time. In which country was he born?

Question Seven
In which year did the Chartered Institute of Bankers receive its royal charter, 1979/1983/1987?

Question Eight

Which university course did Ghislaine Maxwell study at Balliol College, Oxford?

Question Nine
In which year did Margaret Thatcher first become prime minister?

Question Ten
Which movement did Maharishi Mahesh Yogi create in the mid-1950s?

Question Eleven
What did the financial press call the event initiated on 27 October 1985 which made London markets more transparent?

Question Twelve
What innovation did the London Stock Exchange introduce in 1995 for smaller companies?

Question Thirteen
What happened to Hong Kong in June 2001?

Question Fourteen
Which Party Leader won the June 2001 General Election?

Question Fifteen
Which Party Leader said he was turning up the volume?

Question Sixteen
What political event happened in Wales on 12 May 1999?

Question Seventeen
Which US politician was photographed on stage with Sam Bankman-Fried, the founder of the failed crypto currency exchange FTX?

Question Eighteen
Who became prime minister in May 2010?

Question Nineteen
How many air miles is the journey from London to Tokyo?

Question Twenty
When did the United Kingdom legally exit the European Union?

The Square Mile Tales Quiz: ANSWERS

Question One: John Wesley
Question Two: Worcestershire
Question Three: Ian Lavender
Question Four: 1973
Question Five: Lady Ghislaine
Question Six: Pakistan
Question Seven: 1987
Question Eight: Modern History with languages
Question Nine: 4 May 1979
Question Ten: The Transcendental Meditation Foundation
Question Eleven: Big Bang
Question Twelve: The Alternative Investment Market (AIM)
Question Thirteen: It became a Special Administrative Region (SAR) of the People's Republic of China
Question Fourteen: Tony Blair (Labour)
Question Fifteen: Iain Duncan Smith (Conservative)
Question Sixteen: The Welsh Parliament sat for the first time
Question Seventeen: Bill Clinton
Question Eighteen: David Cameron (Conservative)
Question Nineteen: 5,975 miles
Question Twenty: 31 January 2020

And a final thought

At the start of this autobiography I raised the question of approaching old age and the possible consequences.

In early January 2023 I spotted the below article on the BBC website and sent it to some friends with the heading, 'There's hope for us all!'

'A 90-year-old lorry driver from Sheffield is set to carry on trucking for another year after being given a clean bill of health by his doctor. Brian Wilson has chalked up more than 70 years on the road, and

could be the UK's oldest HGV licence-holder.
Like his 1993, 'L-reg' lorry, Mr Wilson also requires a full health
check each year, which he said he passed just before Christmas. He told
the BBC that his GP was 'very pleased' with him.'

My entrepreneur friend Garry Willinge, an Australian now living in Hong Kong and a minister of the Anglican church, with whom I have sat on several boards of directors, responded with a 'thumbs up'. I replied as follows:

On Thu, Jan 12, 2023 at 1:25 AM Tony Drury
<tonydrury39@btinternet.com> wrote:

Garry. In truth, if tomorrow is my last earthly day, I would have no complaints. I'm 76, have known good health most of my life, I've not had to fight any wars, I've known radio, TV, films and the internet plus hours of brilliant sport. My marriage has lasted fifty-four years and my family are all fine. Judy and I have Henry, our grandson, to watch over in the coming years. And I have travelled globally and met people such as yourself.

Not a bad deal.

Tony

***

CHAPTER TWELVE
PUBLISHED IN 2019 ON AMAZON
BOOKS: 'THE FORBIDDEN TATTOO'

In Chapter Eight I made reference to the circumstances leading to the writing of a short story, 'The Forbidden Tattoo'. The colleague who introduced me to the Japanese company Ganapati Plc met a woman at a Christmas drinks party and ended up agreeing to lose a significant amount of weight so that she would then show him a tattoo on her back. It is a true story, promise!

I am lost in admiration for those select few authors who achieve success. It is a brutal challenge chasing the dream of becoming a best-selling writer. It is also full of surprises. Some years ago, I was asked by the managers at Milton Keynes Library to take part in a training session for writers wherein ambitious students were given two weeks to write twenty thousand words on a fictional setting. My role was to suggest how they might approach the challenge and, as I was asked back for several years, can only assume I managed to add value to the sessions.

Following the second year's engagement, a woman, perhaps twenty-five years of age, approached me, handed me a manuscript and asked if I would be willing to read it. I immediately agreed to do so: she was a farmer from Hertfordshire. Her draft work of fiction was desperately in need of editing but, remembering the letter from the lady in Tring (who suggested that her six-year-old son could write better English than me), I drafted a letter to the author praising her efforts and saying how much I enjoyed reading her book (I should have been a full-time politician) and suggesting that a rewrite, including a revision to the chapter when the poachers attacked the farmer in his barn, might pay dividends. I hoped that my letter did not discourage her. Two years later I received a communication from her. She said that my letter was the turning point in her career and she had just landed a contract with a mainstream publishing house.

The preceding chapters in this autobiography have included several references to the subject of my novels, DCI Sarah Rudd, and the five novellas which I have written. Earlier in my career I had a success with my textbook on finance houses. Thus, there has been a degree of satisfaction from writing which has been endorsed by working with the authors at City Fiction.

The world of publishing is vast and yet so much of the activity is simply publishing houses (and film companies) trying to discover the next best-seller and then creating the franchise such as James Bond or Harry Potter. Extraordinary wealth awaits those that succeed.

For the 'also rans', we keep trying!

'The Forbidden Tattoo' which is reproduced below is an attempt to conclude this tale of Square Mile stories in a way which will retain the interest of you, the reader. It was immensely satisfying to write it and then to receive good reviews was a bonus.

The story starts with a series of flashbacks introducing the two central characters: Jack Simpson, a City fund manager with a forty-six-inch waist and swollen feet, and Dr Petrona Chambers who describes herself as 'single but hopeful'. Jack desperately wants to lose some weight and Petra reveals that she has a tattoo on her back. Their chance meeting in a city hotel bar leads to an agreement that if Jack sheds fifty-six pounds, Petra will reveal her tattoo to him. "To do that, I'll have to take off my clothes" she teases her new companion.

But that is just the start of what becomes a complicated situation leading to a final denouement when Jack is forced to see something that defies rational explanation.

The story of 'The Forbidden Tattoo' follows.

THE FORBIDDEN TATTOO

BY

TONY DRURY

Based on a true story

Eight hours ago

Her smile endorsed his enthusiasm. Perhaps it was her green eyes, the powdered bruise on her cheek, her upheld hand.

"Deal," she said.

He knew she meant it.

He put down his glass, knocked the elbow of a fellow drinker in the crowded hotel bar, lifted his podgy fingers and slapped her open palm.

He experienced a surge of anticipation. A crack had appeared in her defences. There was a route by which he was going to be allowed to see her tattoo.

Fourteen hours earlier

Forty-six inch waist and he could not button up the trousers. He shopped at Marks and Spencer because he did not have to try on the clothing in the shop and they always had the best range of men's suits. It was a consequence of their new slimline Italian style tailoring. Never before had he failed to feel comfortable in a forty-six inch waist pair of trousers. He could feel his bum trying to burst out. He'd go back and demand a refund. He would sue the retailer for misleading promotions. His waist measurement was forty-six inches.

He had an important meeting to attend in two hours. The jacket was comfortable. He had put it on in the store. Size XXL. He caught his sixteen-year-old son, Nathan, trying it on. He gave the appearance of having disappeared into a tent.

Eleven hours earlier

The meeting in the City office went well and they won the mandate. He resented it. Four visiting clients and his team of young professionals stealing the limelight. He was in his fifty-first year and older than most of his colleagues. Some were slim by any standard, bursting with life and vitality, and he envied them. Sid, the Finance Director, looked old because he was. He went to sleep halfway through the session and afterwards remembered everything that had been said. Alissa, the head of financial compliance, was naturally provocative. Oxford first, climbed ice-capped mountains, played clarinet in a London-based orchestra and drank pints of real ale. She answered the client's crucial objection with a logic which silenced the room.

She stood up, creatively attracting attention, allowing the male attendees to absorb her physicality. She faced the managing director of their potential client:

"You are asking, Mr Heaton-Hughes, whether we can guarantee an annual return of above seven point three percent over the next five years if you allow us to manage your pension fund."

She paused and straightened her striped jacket.

"For goodness sake, Alissa," he said to himself, "don't say we can, 'cos we can't." His waist was feeling even more uncomfortable as the stress of the meeting was causing his body to swell.

"Mr Heaton-Hughes, we can," Alissa announced and he groaned, inwardly.

"But we might not," she added. "If you can guarantee global interest rates over the next five years and the GDP growth of all the major trading countries, I can give you a more reasoned answer."

He wondered if a button had snapped off as he felt a change in his appearance.

"You are visiting some of our competitors and we have a high regard for them all. So, I get it. You've a challenging decision to make and a great responsibility to your pensioners and workforce to guard their funds as responsibly as you can. I am going to give you five reasons why you should bring your funds to us to manage on your behalf."

He was now perspiring and hugged his jacket around his chest to hide any possible sweat marks.

Alissa asked each of her colleagues to stand up and explain their individual role in the management of pension funds. She ended by announcing that as Compliance Officer, her role was to ensure that every member of the team undertook their responsibilities to the highest professional standards.

"Mr Heaton-Hughes, I want to sum up our approach in one word."

"What word is that?" he asked himself as he felt his feet begin to swell.

"Commitment," Alissa announced. "Commitment to you our client, to our professional standards, to our integrity and, perhaps, most importantly, commitment to the pensioners who will depend upon our competence."

They won the contract, he shook hands with the visitors as they left the building and then watched his team hugging each other. He wished he could embrace Alissa.

His suit was starting to fit a little better as the stitching began to stretch.

Two hours earlier
He concluded checking the draft letter of engagement to their new client and completed the handwritten notes of congratulations to his team. He was thirsty. He locked his office door and nodded to the security officer. It was no longer discussed as it was accepted that he would go the hotel bar for a drink before calling a taxi and going home to fall asleep in the chair in front of the television. He and his wife never spoke about it. There remained a mutual respect and he had a high regard for the way she had nursed her parents into the promised land. They shared the two offspring: Nathan was already an adult in so many ways and his athletics prowess was suggesting Olympian potential. Narisa was lazy and passed her examinations. He sometimes blinked when he remembered she was fourteen years of age but her mother assured him all the pitfalls were covered.

Their relationship was defined by sleeping in separate bedrooms. She, because of noisy adenoids and a growing late-night obsession resulting from her reading of Hilary

Mantel's 'Wolf Hall' and her interest in the Thomas Cromwell trilogy. He, because his body was verging on the repulsive.

They rarely missed their date night: every Thursday, alternately, they booked a restaurant and went out together. They talked and were affectionate although when they arrived home, more often a little the worse for wear, a peck on the cheek was the ultimate in their relationship. Their last dinner was disappointing because they argued the merits of the Liberal Democratic Party and he couldn't think of any. They were beginning to make excuses as to why a week should be missed.

One hour earlier
Tuesday, London, Mayfair, spring. It was relatively quiet and so he sat at the bar. Eddie handed him his drink but he felt uncomfortable. He stood up, tried to ease the pressure around his waist and decided to go over to one of the tables illuminated by ecology efficient powered lighting. He was pleased with the day's progress. Money and wealth were no longer an issue as he had both but he cared about his team and they knew it. He was drinking a large vodka and tonic because it contained fewer calories. He called Eddie over and ordered a pint of strong lager. He'd start the diet on the following Monday.

She came up, looked around the half-empty lounge, and asked if the seat to his right was vacant. She sat down without waiting for an answer. He pretended to be unavailable.

"I've seen you in here before," she said.

He looked at her a little askance.

"I'm not in the mood for talking," he said.

This was not the usual reaction she expected from a middle-aged, over-weight City boss.

"That's a pity."

"I'm a good listener though," he smiled.

She nodded and announced she was going to buy for

167

them a bottle of Prosecco which she brought back to the table with a bowl of dry-roasted peanuts.

"They're full of calories," he said.

"I think your stomach has given up the fight," she suggested.

She lit up their encounter with a compelling smile. She suggested they tell each other a secret about themselves. Jack thought that might be fun. He asked her to begin. She confided that she had two secrets, one of which she'd reveal and the other, only if she enjoyed his company. He poured the wine into their two glasses and shovelled some peanuts into his mouth. He asked her to reveal her first secret.

"I'm an atheist," she said. "I never talk about it. I've looked at the various gods available and none appeals to me."

"Atheist or agnostic?" he asked.

"An agnostic is an atheist without balls," she laughed. "I read that somewhere."

"So what happens when you die?" he asked.

"Pass. I haven't died yet."

She stood up and took off the jacket of her trouser suit. She poured them each another glass of wine. She sat down and crossed her legs: he noted that she was slim.

"Your turn," she said.

He stood up and moved towards the bar.

"Where are you going?" she asked.

"Another bottle of Prosecco. You just told me to get it."

"No, I meant your turn to reveal your secret but as you are up, go and get the bottle: we'll need it."

This was a sound strategy because no sooner had he returned and sat down than he needed to pour the second bottle as she appeared to have drunk the last of the original. He thought his glass had been a third full.

"Give, Mr City Boss. I want to know your secret."

His phone rang and he immediately answered. There then ensued a heated discussion which ended with him accepting her suggestion. He told his guest that she should sit there and wait. She was nonplussed but intrigued. A few minutes later Alissa arrived and sat down at their table. She took out of an envelope she was carrying with her, what appeared to be a six-page foolscap letter. He read it carefully. He asked to see the original. Alissa supplied a similar document marked with red annotations. He read each change and nodded.

"I've tried to keep to your style, Jack, which I love, but the points marked with numbers are definitely breaches of the rules." Alissa ran her hand through her hair. "We have to take out the estimated rate of return. Verboten, sir."

He read again the revised copy, signed it and handed it back to his Compliance Officer. They nodded to each other and she left the hotel lounge to post off the letter to their client.

"Is that your secret?" she laughed. "Bloody attractive."

"I've never noticed," he said. "My secret. If I tell you, it won't be a secret."

"Don't try that on, Mr Jack, City man. Tell all."

Thirty minutes have passed by
He tried to pull himself together but reluctantly undid the buttons on his jacket. He offered her a clue to his proposed revelation but she accused him of delaying tactics.

"I share my secret with Albert Einstein," he announced.

"He was an agnostic," she cried and seemed to hug herself. He noticed that she had taken off her heels. "When he was asked about an afterlife he replied that one life was enough for him."

"I don't wear socks."
She sat back and pondered his words. He told her it was no use trying to look at his feet because he always wore longer trousers that covered his shoes.

"And Einstein did not wear socks?

"The legend is that he thought his big toe would make

a hole in them so he did not wear them." He drank some wine. "In my teens I kept developing rashes on my feet so I simply stopped wearing socks. I wear sandals around the house and at weekends."

"What does your wife say?"

"She forgot about it years ago." The background music was Chopin and some piano pieces. The hotel was filling up. Eddie came over and cleared their table and produced a third bottle of wine although Jack could not remember ordering it. When he went to pay, Eddie shook his head.

"So that's it. You don't wear socks."

"What were you expecting?" he asked.

"I'm a doctor," she said. "I work as a locum. Earn big bucks for three days a week. Crazy but what do I care. I've never had a patient who did not wear socks."

"Am I a patient?"

"If you were, what do you think I should concentrate on?"

"My feet?"

"They're swollen. I spotted that earlier but I never connected the lack of socks. I must be losing my touch."

"What do swollen feet suggest?"

She drank half a glassful of wine and burped.

"Edema, lipedema, diabetes, heart problems, a foot injury, excessive alcoholic intake, venos insufficiency, a blood clot or perhaps you are pregnant." Jack laughed.

"Why don't you and I stop messing around. How much do you weigh?

"Eighteen stone and a few pounds."

"Liar." She paused. "But you must understand you are lying to yourself. I couldn't care a damn what you weigh."

"Eighteen stone and a few pounds," he repeated.

She slipped on her heels, stood up, straightened her trousers and told Jack to follow her. Which he did. They exited the hotel lounge and took a lift to a lower ground floor where she led him into the member's gym. There was a black guy in a white tracksuit. She threw her arms around his neck, handed him a twenty pound note and told Zademe, as the label on his uniform announced, that she wanted him to do her a favour. She asked him to take Jack into the changing rooms, undress and weigh him, allow him to shower and then bring him back to her. Zademe was instructed to keep the weighing result to himself until he came back to her.

Thirty-five minutes later Zademe and a pristine-looking City man returned. She asked the gym attendant to write down the weight. She looked at the slip of paper and told Jack they were returning back to the lounge bar. They spotted Eddie. He had retained their half-empty bottle of wine and they settled back into the hotel atmosphere.

"Eighteen stone and a few pounds," she said.

"I wasn't lying. You owe me an apology."

"You can have it in pounds, stone and pounds or kilograms," she said.

"Which sounds better?" he laughed.

"Let's try two hundred and sixty-eight pounds," she suggested.

Jack took out his phone and used his calculator app. He went very quiet.

"There must be a mistake. Zademe was rather casual."

"Do you want to go and challenge him?" she asked. Eddie came over.

"Petra," he said. "He'll meet you at The Ivy at nine." She thanked Eddie.

"Petra," said Jack.

"Doctor Petrona Chambers," she said. "That's my name. Single but hopeful."

"Can you help me lose weight?" he pleaded.

"No. I can't. It has to come from you. Inside you. Losing weight is one of the most painful experiences facing a human being. Your body expects to be supplied a certain amount of food each day to enable you to carry around all that weight." She paused. "You might last a few days on a restricted calorie regime but then Alissa will come into your office with a problem and that evening you'll come to the bar and drink too much. You'll go home and eat burgers and chips and tell yourself you'll start the diet the next day."

"Nineteen stone," he gasped as he looked at his phone. "Nineteen stone and two pounds. One hundred and twenty-one kilograms. What I am going to do?" he asked.

"Probably die sooner than you wish, possibly painfully. There are a few who get away with it but that's playing with fire. There are endless possibilities. Diabetes and you'll end up having your feet amputated. Your knees and hips will have to be replaced. Heart issues. The list is endless."

"If I lose weight...?"

"You have to lose weight, Jack. It's never too late and worth a shot. You're stinking rich. Go and pay a private doctor to give you a medical and get your prostate checked." She laughed. "Did you know that an antidote to prostate problems is an active sex life?"

"I'll have my prostate checked."

Present time

"I've been thinking," said Petra. "There may be a way I can help you lose weight." He gripped the edge of the chair.

"I have a second secret. If I tell you my second secret it might help you lose weight."

"Do your patients ever understand what you are talking about?"

"Probably not," she laughed. "My secret is that I have a tattoo on my back. It took several weeks and was painful but I love it."

"Where on your back?" asked Jack.

"That's part of the secret," she smiled.

"I'm obese, I'm tired, I'm deflated and I've not the vaguest idea what you are talking about."

"You lose fifty-six pounds in weight and I'll show you my tattoo." She paused. To do that I'll have to take off my clothes." He knocked over his glass of wine. They became involved in an animated conversation as he pressed her on the details of the challenge. She meant it. He believed her. She held up her hand.

"Deal," she said. He slapped her open palm.

"Deal," he said. "Fifty-six pounds," he repeated to himself.

He then realised she had gone. He picked up a piece of paper from the table. It was her card. She had written on it, 'Two days. 7.00.'

Day one: the medical
The doctor removed his gloved finger from his anus.

"The old ways are the best ways. I can check your prostate with a blood test but I prefer to feel it. We'll tick that box, Mr Simpson. No prostate problems."

On receiving further directions he went and stood on the surgery scales. He then lay down on the examination couch and was prodded and poked. An ECG followed the taking of his blood pressure. Then he ran on the indoor running machine and breathed into a plastic pipe.

He dressed and sat in front of the medical examiner.

"Why are you here, Mr Simpson?" He looked down at his notes. "You've not drawn my attention to any particular symptoms."

"I want to lose weight," said Jack.

"Why?" asked the GP.

"My clothes are too tight," he suggested.

"No problem. You're not going to tell me. It's usually another woman but that's nothing to do with me. Just wait outside for an hour or so. The blood tests will be through and we can have a chat."

Jack was reading a copy of the November 2018 edition of 'The Lady' when he was called back in to the consulting room. The doctor was poring over charts and test results. He sat down.

"Well now, Mr Simpson, good news. You are in pretty good health. My professional indemnity insurers insist I caveat that with pages of warnings that I might be wrong

173

and no medical is foolproof." He smiled and drank some cold coffee. "But hey, it's a lovely day outside and your test results are encouraging. I can go on for hours about the details and in fact I will. I'll write to you with a full report."

"Please send it to my office," interrupted Jack.

"Yes. Noted. I suggest you take it to your GP. He'll probably want to put you on statins. Your main cholesterol reading is a bit high. But overall, a good result. Now we must discuss your weight…" Jack stood up and headed for the exit.

"I'll deal with that," he said.

"At least four stone off, Mr Simpson, and please don't delay."

"We all seem to be in agreement about that," smiled Jack.

"Mr Simpson, do I send my invoice to your office?"

Day two: Petra

"Mr City Boss Jack, I'm impressed, you've had a medical," she said, as she sipped an orange juice. He looked askance at her choice of refreshment. She waved the glass in the air. She told him it was his fault. She had arrived at The Ivy a little pickled and had a blazing row with her brother.

"He's on his way out," she said. "We share a house, in truth my house, but he's got gambling debts."

"Have you been locuming today?" asked Jack. Eddie came over with a bottle of wine and she was soon imbibing. She put her hand on his knee. He noticed her light-blue jeans.

"I helped a patient today. What did I do?"

Jack was trying not to stare at the birthmark on her cheek. It was there in all its glory tonight: no powder covering.

"Aren't you supposed to help your patients?" he asked. Petra laughed and Jack shuffled around on his seat.

"Creams, pills, sickness notes and so on: I suppose they matter. Many of my patients get, "Take the prescription and if you don't feel better come back in seven days." She chuckled and Jack moaned inwardly. "That means that I have no idea what is wrong with you. That is why I am an atheist. If there is a god, how could he create a world with so much pain?" She smoothed down her jeans. "What did I do today to help a patient?" Jack admitted he had no idea. She told him that she syringed a patient's ears.

"Elderly man came in. Obviously in some discomfort. Said he had a brain tumour. He ears were waxed up so I syringed them. Usually we ask a nurse to help but I was feeling good today so I did it myself. The one ear was tough: the wax had hardened but we won. It will take a few days for the ears to fully recover but my patient left feeling like a spring lamb and I felt good." She stood up, played around with her clothes and sat down again.

"How did you get from a brain tumour to blocked ears?" asked Jack and then allowed her to pull his nose.

"Mr City Moneyman, six years of the best medical training available in the world, dedication and my special ability to diagnose."

"Oh," said Jack.

"Also, he was stone deaf and couldn't hear a word I said." Jack laughed.

"You've had a medical?" she continued as she picked up their opening comments. "What did the doctor tell you?"

"I'm overweight by four stone."

"It's more than that but he's smart. What he did was assess what you might try to achieve without changing your basic physiology. It breaks my heart when I treat people who lose weight and then put back on even more pounds."

"As far as I could tell he did not have a tattoo on his back."

" What else did he say. Did he test your prostate?"

"How come you have a tattoo on your back?" asked Jack.

Day three: planning the diet

"We posted your medical report to you yesterday, Mr Simpson, together with my invoice, to your office. I hope we haven't done anything wrong?" Jack remained grim-faced. He looked around the surgery which was immaculately tidy.

"May I ask why you are here, again?"

"How do I lose weight?" asked Jack, as he rubbed his perspiring brow. "Fifty-six bleedin' pounds of the stuff." Dr Lucking leaned back in his chair and smiled.

"I earn pots of money answering that question, Mr Simpson, and most of my patients fail to lose any weight. Some shed a few pounds but put them back and add more. It's possibly the most difficult question a doctor ever has to address." He drank some water. "It's a medical conundrum because the answer is quite straight forward."

"Which is what?"

"Eat less."

"I'm paying you to hear that?" snapped Jack.

"I can dress it up and talk about the food consumption/bodily needs equation, or I can extoll the virtues of the Atkins diet, or the 5/2 regime; perhaps you'd like to hear about the Volumetics Diet, or I give you an application form to join Weight Watchers. Perhaps you should go and live in Spain and follow the Mediterranean menu, lots of oils."

"Are you taking me seriously?" asked Jack.

"Yes, Mr Simpson, I am taking you very seriously. You need to lose four stone or fifty-six pounds if you prefer. The odds are, you won't. Few people lose weight. Do you understand what I am saying. I am treating you seriously. You are a successful City operator: I've looked you up and perhaps you might like to advise me on my pension investments." Jack looked askance.

"Your medical was surprisingly robust: you're in good shape. Read my report and see your doctor about your cholesterol levels. But you need to lose a lot of weight if you want to spend your pension. To lose weight, you need to eat less and it's one of the hardest of all human challenges which is why obesity is a national catastrophy. It's wrecking the NHS. It's not just heart and circulatory problems. It's orthopedic: we are putting in new joints every day. Walk down the High Street and observe the numbers of people using mobility chairs and who are on sticks and crutches. The cause is usually because their bodies have had to carry too much weight."

"How many of your patients have lost weight permanently?" asked Jack.

"A few. Sometimes it's simply the truth. If I tell a person they will die within say a year, they might do something about it. To be honest it's probably too late for them but we'll never stop trying."

"Is that it?"

"As I hinted to you. I've a few male patients who have taken up with a younger woman. Sometimes the pure fulfilment of finding love will provide the spur they need."

"How do I eat less?" asked Jack.

"The best way I've seen, and, in fact, had some success with, is the South Beach diet. It was evolved by an American cardiologist who used the low glycemic index. This measures blood glucose levels and is important because excessive weight is the result of the body storing sugar. He worked out the index values of all carbohydrates which are the foods with sugar content."

"Explain what that means to me?" instructed Jack.

"Cut out potatoes, bread and wheat-associated foods, rice and pasta."

"That's it?"

"And walk six miles a day. That will use up about four-hundred calories." He sipped his glass of water. "When you break your diet, which you will, don't panic. Your body is quite forgiving. You must go back to the regime the next day."

"I'll lose weight?" The doctor nodded.

"How long to lose fifty-six pounds?" asked Jack.

The medical practitioner thought about his question. He said that if Jack maintained the discipline, even with the odd blemish, it might take as little as twenty, perhaps twenty-five weeks. He suggested keeping to small amounts of white wine and definitely no beers or lagers. Jack stood up. Doctor Lucking asked if he might ask a personal question. In response to Jack's wave of his hand, he wondered why his client did not wear socks.

"Because," he replied. "I think I am Albert Einstein." He stood up and moved towards the door.

"Shall I send my invoice to your office?" asked Dr Lucking as he scratched his head.

The story of the tattoo

Dr Petrona Chambers had been qualified for seven years. She loved her work, despised her brother's weaknesses, and relished the five months she had taken out to see the world. She reached Australia, travelled in a convoy up through Queensland, found a lover, ditched him, reached the Phillipines, worked for two months to replenish her cash reserves, went west to Cambodia, spoke to her mother every few days, suffered a week of food poisoning, needed antibiotics for a rash on her inside thigh, recovered and reached Vietnam from where she was to fly back to Britain to begin work as a locum doctor.

She thought that Ho Chi Minh City was congested, noisy, polluted and dangerous. Her health was fully restored and she felt libidinous. They met in a hotel bar, drank rather too much before they went to bed, where upon he announced he could not accept her situation. She cried, showered and started to walk the streets as she struggled to accept his rejection.

It was called 'Saigon Ink' and was off a main road in a parade of upmarket shops. It was colourful, pictorial and welcoming. The placards proclaimed prizes won at conventions in Thailand and in Bangkok. She entered the tattoo salon and was asked for evidence that she could pay. Her sense of caution evaporated as she handed over some American dollars. She was introduced to Binh Nguyen, who she liked.

He spoke no English so their communications were by hand. It was established that she wanted it on her back. She selected the eleventh picture she was shown and, eventually, Binh understood the changes she wanted made to the original. She took off her clothes and lay on the table. Binh took a step back and gazed at her body: he used his light touch to establish the area to be covered. It took longer than she expected and she was required to pay over more US dollars.

Perhaps Petra should have been a little more careful because when she used mirrors to view her tattoo, her hand flew to her mouth. It was bigger than expected or commissioned. She adored it. It contained the message she wanted to express to the world.

With the exception of a medical associate, nobody else had yet seen her tattoo. She returned to England, began work, went to a hotel bar and met Jack Simpson. She was keen to get a reaction and chose her victim carefully. The balance that he had to lose four stone in weight appealed to her sense of fair play.

False start
It was Friday: Sid, the Finance Director was off work with stress, Alissa was wearing a brown skirt and black boots, the quarterly profits were up by sixteen percent and it was three days before Jack was due to start his diet. He called in at the hotel dreaming Petra would be there but ended up talking to a know-all from somewhere: perhaps the southern States of America. He knew about everything: the Six Sigma business process introduced by General Electric in the 1990s which revolutionised production to new heights, where President Trump had hidden all his off-shore money, the truth about the final days of Marilyn Monroe, and that

was after only the second glass of bourbon. Jack had to admit he did not know the difference between his drink and whisky. Alexander III did. "Fella, Scotch is whisky made in yon hills in Scotland and comes from malted barley, and bourbon, the real stuff, is whiskey with an 'e' and comes from Kentucky where my grand-daddy was born. He emptied his glass and added that it was distilled from corn.

Jack decided that was enough and lost the plot trying to explain to Alexander III about his diet. "Jack, fella, this is Paul Newman territory. The Royal Marine Commando diet is for you." Nature came to his rescue because Alexander III had to visit the facilities and Jack hit Google. On his return the American was informed that Paul Newman, in the film 'Cool Hand Luke', set in a sadistic Florida prison farm, ate fifty eggs.

How this translated into the Royal Marine Commando diet never became clear because Alexander III stood up, shook his hand and walk out of the lounge bar. Jack researched the diet and discovered that remarkable weight loss results could be achieved by just eating eggs. The next day he had three hard-boiled eggs for breakfast, three poached eggs for lunch and three scrambled eggs for dinner. Avril Simpson had never before known her husband so enthusiastic about going shopping.

At two in the morning Jack Simpson was ill and rather sick. The following morning he revisited Dr Lucking's recommendations and settled for a diet which was to begin on Monday.

Two weeks later (part one)
"Jack, you're da man," yelled Zademe as he screamed out the reading from the digital scales. "You ditched twelve pounds of da porridge." He stood up and punched Jack in the stomach. "Two five six, man." He slapped him on his back. "You go and tell de Pussy your news."

The dieter converted the verbal outpouring into eighteen stone, four pounds. He let the towel drop to the ground and went into the shower. After drying himself, he headed for the hotel lounge: he felt a million pounds.

Petra was sipping a glass of wine and looking at her mobile. As Jack reached her, she told him that life was unfair. It transpired that the surgery where she was working as a locum had called her back in the following morning. She explained that she had intended sleeping for twelve hours and then having her hair washed and cut.

"I'm a fool to myself," she said. "I care too much. I called a woman back because I was worried I had misdiagnosed her symptoms. I hadn't but she had to go to hospital when I found a growth she didn't even know about." She looked up. "Wow!" she exclaimed. She poured him a glass of wine and suggested he had lost a stone in weight. She became rather professional and demanded to know his secret. He explained that he was eating sensibly, drinking very little, walking six miles every evening and he wanted to see her tattoo.

"And so you shall, Jack. Three stone to go and don't forget I'll be checking with Zademe to ensure you're not fiddling." She reached across and pulled his trousers away from his stomach. "Ha!" she exclaimed, "The evidence is clear cut. Well done Mr City Moneyman." She lifted her head and kissed him.

The previous fourteen days

The Irish theologian and philosophic author of fiction, C S Lewis, wrote that 'the safest road to hell is the gradual one – the gentle slope, soft underfoot, without sudden turnings, without milestones, without signposts.'

The nineteen stone, two pounds of Jack Simpson bypassed these safety checks and dived straight into a daily inferno. Twenty years earlier, he had given up smoking. That was simple. Stop smoking, accept the withdrawal symptoms and wait for normality to gradually return. The crucial psychological element was that there was no option. Just one puff of a cigarette and the nicotine addiction returned with the additional consequence that trying again a few days later was even harder.

From one minute past midnight on day one of his diet he realised that one lapse, despite what Dr Lucking had advised, could be fatal. He had devised a daily menu consisting of fresh melon and a piece of wholemeal bread with a thin spread of butter for breakfast. Lunch, and so often that would be with clients, was either steamed fish and salad or boiled or roasted chicken with a tomato and onion mix. He was allowed two small glasses of white wine, every twenty-four hours. If he wished he was permitted a yoghurt at any time. In the evening, he could have eggs and/or fish with leafy green vegetables or cauliflower. He compiled the regime himself.

He faced two challenges. From the start, every night, his stomach groaned and he became obsessed with the thought of oil based and/or fatty foods. He had to drag himself past MacDonald's. On the second evening he went into the kitchen and made himself a ham sandwich, laden with butter. He held it up to his mouth and then rushed into the garden and threw it over the fence towards the railway line.

He bought himself a pedometer wrist watch and spent well over half an hour reading the instructions. He dismissed the step counter as he only wanted to know two readings: how far had he walked and how many calories had he expended? After various calculations he arrived at the answer that, at his current weight, over six miles he would lose around four hundred calories.

His first solo excursion around the local park took two hours to complete the target distance and used up three hundred and seventy-eight calories. He was absolutely drained and, as he took off his newly-purchased pair of trainers, he discovered a blister under his large toe.

The household tensions increased by the day as Avril suspected an affair and Nathan and Narisa couldn't stop laughing as, each evening, their father collapsed through the front door. Avril took exception to the change in washing she was expected to undertake and started throwing away his briefs which contained pungent stains and smells. Then she remembered that her husband did not wear socks and, unbeknown to him, smelt his walking shoes. Her head jerked back: she applied a liberal spray of deodorant.

After four evenings it was mutually agreed that a family crisis meeting should be convened. Avril added to her list of complaints that she had no idea what meals to prepare. Nathan had discovered the pedometer and asked his father if he was training to be an astronaut.

"Sorry, Team Simpson," said Jack, as he sipped his second permitted glass of wine while wiping the perspiration off his forehead. "I have been selfish." Avril nodded and drank her gin and tonic. "I've had a medical examination and although I'm fit, I've been told to lose four stone in weight as a matter of some importance." He absorbed the hushed response. Avril reddened and asked why she had not been consulted? Narisa announced that she thought her father was twenty stone. Nathan played with his mobile phone. "That's bloody fifty-six pounds: you'll never do it."

"I will because I want to see the tattoo," thought Jack.

"When did you go to the surgery?" asked Avril. "My friend Janette is on reception and she would have mentioned it to me."

"We have a private practice which we use for medical cases within the business. I went there."

"How heavy are you, Dad?" asked Narisa.

"Nineteen stone and two pounds. Well, I was on Monday. I will weigh in every week."

"Our bathroom scales are unreliable," suggested Narisa. "I'm a kilogram lighter than the reading they give me."

"Your bum is fat," said Nathan. Their mother separated the warring children.

"There's a gym near to the office. I will be weighing in

there, once a week."

Avril could not understand this development and suggested it would be easier if her husband weighed himself at home. The issue dissipated as conflict broke out again due to Nathan's objecting to his sister changing channels on the television. The evening moved on although it was obvious that Avril was disturbed. She limited her anguish to demanding she be told of her husband's future dietary requirements. She added that if he could occasionally get back at a reasonable time, it would help her in starting the culinary preparations.

The first week staggered on and Jack decided not to weigh in until the following Monday. Petra was not available that week and so a meeting two weeks after the start of the self-discipline was agreed.

The evening walk proved far more arduous than expected. Jack was walking at at about three miles per hour and his circuits round the local park were taking just under two hours. His leg muscles were proving decidedly unhelpful as they rebelled again the unexpected regime. His Achilles tendon became sore and his lower back protested. As he slowly improved and, after two weeks, reduced the timing to one hour forty minutes, he became bored. He purchased a cassette player with headphones and listened to Jamie Cullum. But his concentration was fragile because he found himself thinking of the tattoo and the body on which it was located. As the pounds began to disappear, he was becoming more alert and started to feel younger.

Two weeks later (part two)
"Yes and no," was the answer to his question.

Petra was rather cuddly. Jack asked her if she was reacting as a doctor or whether she was seeing him in another way. The question was rewarded with a hug. She answered by explaining that she relished achievement. She emphasized how diffficult it is for individuals to lose weight and so she was simply acknowledging his success. She rubbed her cheek. Jack had heard her views on weight loss a number of times but, by now, if Petra repeated the two times arithmetic table, he would be enthralled.

"Can I ask you a personal question?" he asked.

"Yes, you can," she replied. "I'll decide whether I'm going to answer it."

"Why do you powder the bruise on your face?" Dr Petra Chambers lifted her glass to her lips, sipped some wine and put it down again.

"It's a form of congenital dermal melanocytosis," she said. "It's a birthmark."

"Oh," said Jack.

"The common name for it is a Mongolian Spot. It occurs when skin pigment gets trapped in the deeper layers. It's rather unusual but that's life. I wish my breasts were bigger, but they're not."

That was the end of the diet for the day. Jack rushed to the bar and returned with a bottle of his favourite white wine. He poured the Chablis into two clean glasses.

"If you don't repent tomorrow and go through dietary pain I'll operate on your testicles," suggested Petra and then she started to cry. Jack sat back, took a deep breath and chastised himself: Mongolian Spots, small breasts or the threat to operate on his anatomy? He put his hand on her thigh. Her joggers felt warm and she placed her fingers over his.

"This is the first time as an adult, outside doctors, that I have ever talked about my birthmark," she explained, as the tears continued to fall. My mother denied its existence, my father ignored it and friends never mention it."

She wiped her eyes and poured some more wine into their glasses.

"I've spoken to several consultants. The Spots, as they are called, normally disappear as a child grows into adolescence. Mine has stayed behind. Operating is almost impossible and would leave blemishes."

He pondered her response which made no sense.

There was virtually nothing these days that the medical world could not accomplish. His business managed the pension fund of a private medical consortium based in Edinburgh and, over the years, Jack had become familiar with some of their achievements.

"Does the powder help?" he asked.

"Pure vanity," she said. "If I was advising a patient I would suggest ignoring it and get on with the rest of your life."

"So, take your own advice," suggested Jack.

"I'm a bad patient," laughed Petra. "Hell, I'm just waiting for the man of my dreams to sweep me off my feet."

"Is there a weight limit?" asked Jack.

"You're heavily married. Don't be silly." She paused. "No weight limit but he'll have to accept small breasts."

"They can operate on those," teased Jack.

"They're small and they're staying small." She finished the bottle of wine. "There are plenty of other areas of interest."

Jack groaned as he spilt the few remaining splashes of wine over his trousers.

Another month has passed

Zademe hugged his client: he decided to double-check the digital reading.

In his inimitable way he announced that Jack had broken the seventeen stone barrier. They decided to repeated the exercise. He stood naked and breathed out deeply before stepping back onto the platform. Zademe went down on his knees, played around with his fingers, leaped up and told the world that Jack was sixteen stone and thirteen pounds, a total loss of thirty one pounds. He suggested that Jack go and tell de Pussy the news. Zameme was putting aside the money that Jack was giving him. It now totalled over four hundred pounds, half of which was being sent to his mother in Trinidad. It would help pay for her treatment.

Jack had changed tailors and was now wearing eight-hundred-pound City suits. He sat down in the hotel lounge and watched as Petra put her fruit juice back down on the table. She moved a glass towards her companion. The background music was Led Zeppelin which made a change from Andrew Lloyd Webber.

"My father always dressed smartly but you're setting new standards Mr City mogul." She smiled. "He was in the Civil Service and I spent my early years in Singapore and Hong Kong." She laughed. "My father was a bit naughty. I should have taken the advice I was given and undergone a DNA test." She paused. "Jack, can you please forget I said that."

*

In the four weeks that had elapsed leading up to the sensational news of his breaking the seventeen stone barrier, he had met Petra nearly every Tuesday evening in the hotel bar after the weigh-in. Each occasion was different; she was sometimes driven by sessions in the surgery and would reflect on events. A girl of eight was wrongly diagnosed by another doctor and died three days later in hospital. Petra was not involved but seemed to take it personally. She confided to Jack that if the parents had brought the child to her, their daughter would probably be alive today. "He drinks," she told Jack. "The senior partner will cover up for him."

Jack was finding that the world was treating him differently. He was changing. He now wore socks. He went to the barber's shop every week for a haircut and shave. For the first time he had his eyebrows trimmed. He spent some time choosing an aftershave which he adopted as his own. It was noticed by others. He always wore a white shirt and a striped tie. Rather old school but it was elegant. He was paying four hundred and fifty pounds for his shoes.

The atmosphere in the office was changing. Sid, the

Finance Director, had taken his retirement package which Jack increased by a substantial sum. On the last day they held each other: it was the end of a fifteen-year partnership without rancour. His replacement was Hector. It was a name which was ready made for office humour except that Hector was not having it. At six foot four-and-a-bit inches and a lot of muscle he was in a powerful position to deter the humourists. Of course, Billy, a trainee actuary, did not heed the warnings and, one Friday, exited the men's facilities looking decidedly the worse for wear. Hector was good at his job. He had trained with an American Finance Group and spent two years in New York. He and Alissa could not take their eyes off each other.

Jack become increasing aware that he was changing, for the better, and he was enjoying far less tension in his life. More of his colleagues became willing to enter into his office and ask for his advice. There was a City scandal in progress concerning illiquid investments: shares in more risky companies that were difficult to sell. Jack knew the parties and, as always, the guilty would walk away richer and the financial regulator, five years too late, would announce a review.

Hector was not having that. He emailed a detailed instruction to all the investment teams announcing that he would be launching daily checks and if he found any risky investment situations the manager would be answering to him. Jack called him into his office.

"Hector, I applaud the initiative, but you can't do this. Your job is finance."

Hector stood up and Jack wondered what might happen. He placed three files on his boss's desk.

"I know that Sid was a personal friend, Mr Simpson, but his systems were shit. Have you any idea how near you have been to breaching Financial Conduct Authority capital rules?"

"Well, I have been instigating…"

"The first file covers our internal systems: there is

much reorganisation needed and I require your authorisation to contract with these people; they're the best and can revamp us in six weeks. Please sign here." He looked down at the capital expenditure authority: two million and a few hundred pounds. He signed the form.

"The second file concerns authorisations. I am breaking the senior team into six. Every decision within the medium- and high-risk categories must be signed off by three category AA individuals."

Jack stared at the flow charts. At the top of each channel was Hector.

"Where am I?" asked the Chief Executive.

"Out for lunch," replied Hector. "Without you, the business dies. We must increase our flow of new business." Hector pushed the third file in front of him. Jack opened the cover.

"These are the monthly accounts. From now on you will receive them three days before the Board Meeting. Please go to page four. Jack turned to the analysis of capital adequacy.

"Sid made a fundamental error in the way he recognised Research and Development expenditure. There is a thirty million pound adjustment to be made. I have met with our auditors and they have moved the partner responsible away from our account. I have invited our new accountant, Mrs Angela Ridding, to come and meet you next week."

Jack put his hands in his head and groaned. Thirty million pounds. The Regulator will be here in hours and the heavy mob will be crawling over every part of his organisation. He looked down again at page four. Where was the thirty million pound correction?"

"The Regulator could suspend us, Hector," he agonised.

"Why would he do that, Mr Simpson?"

"Thirty million pounds wrongly shown?"

"It's in our favour. It's a credit. I'm adding back fifteen

million this quarter and two more add-backs of seven and a half million will follow. The auditors have signed off my file and I've spoken to the Regulator. Alissa and I are being interviewed next week but they've already told me that they're impressed with the moves you've masterminded."

"Well, yes, Hector, I had realised that changes were needed and you have covered many of the areas I have been reviewing." His shirt was clinging to his skin. "I'm pleased to see that you've actioned my ideas." He paused. "Hector. Just one thing. We can't afford to lose Alissa." His office door opened and in came Alissa wearing a pink dress promoted by a TV personality.

"Hi Jack," she beamed. "I'm claiming Hector. We're going out for lunch and he's paying."

As they left, their boss wondered why Hector called him 'Mr Simpson'.

*

At home, nothing changed. Narisa and Nathan lived their adolescent lives, had the occasional fight and discussed Franz Kafka. Narisa accused her brother of skim-reading. Nathan, by describing his disgust at Grete Samsa's rejection of her brother, Gregor, changing into a giant insect, showed that he had absorbed the social commentary within 'The Metamorphosis'. Narisa retorted that his view was influenced by his paranoic hatred of sisters.

Avril Simpson continued her individual pathway and never failed to appreciate her surroundings and lifestyle. She had a clear calculation as to when the children would no longer require her immediate support. Then there would be changes. She continued to enjoy the weekly date-nights and silently laughed at her husband's ordering of steamed whole plaice and a green salad. She purposely refused to acknowledge his loss of weight and the change in his appearance. She would think to herself: "I hope she's good in bed." When they returned home there was no longer even the hint of a hug as they went to their separate bedrooms.

Earlier times

Jack Simpson had never seen life as a popularity contest. His entrepreneurial drive led to the success of his fund-management business. As the good times arrived, there was a period when the children added so much, their parents struggled into their old age and died and the social environment was stimulating, especially Beth next door. He added his zest to the local Conservative Party although he rejected the idea of a committee role. Their Member of Parliament worked hard to develop a relationship and Jack was happy to meet him in London for lunch. With his agreement, he fed back to the Treasury the various scandals taking place. He sensed nobody wanted to know. He knew of five members of the House of Lords who were taking the notion of personal corruption to new levels, but he didn't care. His philosophy was that if the guilty peers were exposed, five more would take their place.

Beth, their neighbour with the tedious schoolteacher husband, had seductive thighs. Jack studied the female form with some commitment. He didn't do porn because he had no need. He was an intensely family man and Avril was fun. She could eat anything and stay slim.

Then changes began to appear: there was no logic. Jack became frustrated with his body. He had always been able to lose weight and every January, after the seasonal excesses, he de-camped to the squash club where he removed around ten pounds. He played the Ladies' number one and couldn't beat her. He perfected a drop shot into the corner of the court which, in her efforts to retrieve the ball, resulted in Connie bending almost double and revealing the most rewarding pair of knickers. The occasional dinner party with Beth and her husband usually ended up with Jack dreaming.

When he turned forty, the squash court became more demanding, Connie left for Iceland and Jack could not shift the weight. Worse was to follow. Fourteen stone passed by and he bought some new scales which confirmed the approached fifteen-stone barrier. One weekday afternoon, Avril had a consultant's appointment and Jack worked from home. He ran out of milk and, without thinking, called round next door to ask for some help. He found the front door was open and the bell was not working and so he went in and reached the kitchen.

Beth showed no surprise. He looked at her bikini top and the briefest of shorts. Her thighs were golden following their family two weeks' holiday in Egypt.

"Jack!" she exclaimed. "Now I have you all to myself." She rushed to the front door which she locked from the inside. Forty minutes later, as she looked into his face when the moment of fulfillment arrived, she uttered a moan of contentment.

"I've always fancied you, Jack," she said, nibbling his ear. Two months later Jack and Avril moved into separate bedrooms.

Jack and Petra
"No, your target is fifteen stone, two pounds." Petra wiped her lips. "You started at nineteen stone, two pounds. Today you are sixteen stone, thirteen pounds: you have another twenty-five pounds to go."

"I thought we agreed three stone?" lied Jack.

"When you reach fifteen stone, two pounds, all will be revealed."

"I'll be allowed to see your tattoo?" pleaded Jack.

"Oh yes," replied Petra. She sipped her orange juice and silently pleaded with Jack to lose the remaining pounds. She so wanted to show him her tattoo.

Five more weeks have flown by
Zademe beamed and pocketed the cash. His mother was improving but the drugs were expensive. When Jack achieved his weight loss, he had plans for him. They agreed the scales were showing fifteen stone and twelve pounds.

There had been a period when Jack started to struggle but made the sensible decision to ask Zademe his advice. The six miles' walk was reduced to two and swimming was introduced: ten lengths in a session and then twenty minutes in the steam room. But the best was to come: Zademe introduced Jack into the boxing ring and he took to it like a duck to water. Zademe found him Henry who was large. He had once boxed at a serious level and had the ability to move Jack around the ring without hurting him. One one occasion Jack hit him with an exceptional swinging punch and, for a fleeting moment, Henry angered. He tapped Jack on his chin as a warning.

Zademe made his move. He stated the obvious. The dieter had ten more pounds to lose and then his target was achieved. Zademe asked if he could become Jack's personal trainer and he made a rather telling point. He asked if, after all the effort needed to lose four stone, Jack wanted to take the risk of putting the weight back on. This was exactly what Jack had been thinking. A deal was done which included Jack confirming his full membership of the gym. Zademe was to be paid seven hundred pounds a month into his bank account starting immediately. Within four days Zademe's bank had accepted a standing order instruction to pay to a bank account in the West Indies, three hundred pounds every month. Within three months the additional medicines and attention from the doctor resulted in his mother walking without her sticks.

Petra disappeared for a week and so their next Tuesday meeting was when Jack had lost another two pounds. He was furious and Zademe had to literally pull him out of the steam room.

Petra had a facial tan but Jack decided not to invade her privacy. They celebrated seeing each other by indulging in a bottle of house white wine.

"Eight pounds to go, Jack," said Petra.

"How will you show me your tattoo?" asked Jack. She put her hand to her mouth.

"I hadn't thought of that," she suggested.

Alissa is assaulted

It all went wrong at work for Jack. He knew something was amiss but had lost, in Sid, his confidante. Alissa was due holiday and so her absence was accepted. Hector was different. The financial reports were coming through and a letter from the financial regulator confirmed their satisfaction with the recent developments. The new computer system was being installed and the general reaction of the investment teams was positive. Hector was wearing the same clothes two or three days' running and he needed a haircut. Jack was walking round the office and his eyes alighted on Billy. The look was troubling. He knew something.

He stayed late to review the latest investment performances. His office door opened and Alissa entered. Jack leaped up, grabbed a chair and sat her down. He reached for a glass of water and handed it to her. As she began to settle down he asked if she wanted to remove her shades. The one eye was closed and the other bloodshot.

"Hector?" he asked. She nodded as the tears started to pour down her face. Jack lifted his phone. He spoke to the senior partner of a rather expensive firm of lawyers. Within thirty minutes another lawyer arrived with a woman colleague. She asked them to leave her with Alissa. Jack and his adviser left the room and sat down with a carafe of water.

"Glad you contacted us, Jack. These are the vital moments. You would not believe how these cases can go wrong."

"All that matters is Alissa," responded Jack.

"Not so, you're assuming guilt and that is dangerous. You have no evidence it was this man, Hector." He paused. "If it was, what steps are you going to take to protect your staff?" Lawyer Daisy Hamblin came out.

"Call an ambulance, John. It's sexual. I want her in

hospital before we call in the police."

The next few days passed in turmoil before the facts were established. Hector confessed to an attempted rape which, when his previous history emerged, was all he could do. The two partners of the agency which had recruited Hector were never to forget their meeting with Jack Simpson.

He spent all his free time with his colleagues. The law firm arranged for every member of staff to be interviewed. Three received counselling although it became clear nothing had happened in the office environment. Hector had a breakdown and the legal process took its course.

Jack sat with with Alissa in the lounge of her temporary home eighty miles to the west of London. He knew from the specialist who had been asked to ensure she receive the best care possible, that physically she had recovered from her internal injuries. Her mother brought in a tray of tea and then disappeared. As she left she squeezed Jack's shoulder.

"We can't wait for you to come back," said Jack, as he resisted the chocolate cake.

"You know that isn't going to happen, Jack, don't you?"

"Yes, I know that, but I had to try." He paused. "Alissa, I'm not very good at this sort of thing. I'm rather a selfish person."

"I think you are the loveliest man that I've ever met, apart from my father."

"Any plans?" asked Jack. "Before you answer, here is a letter telling you of your financial settlement." Alissa read the details and gulped.

"That is rather generous, Jack, thank you."

"Plans?"

"I'll take time out," she said.

"And that is the wrong decision," said Jack. Alissa stared at him and explained that she was scared. He responded by asking her how she was going to find out about the future. Her head sunk. She said she was receiving so much advice it was overwhelming. Jack stood up and fetched a package he had left on the hall table.

"You remember our client in Scotland. The medical consortium. They came down to see us. They asked where you were? We did not tell them. The managing director then asked permission to approach you. He wants a compliance officer at assistant director level. I told him, in confidence, about your situation. He never blinked. They want you, Alissa." He handed her the package. Jack got up and went over to her. She stood up and they hugged each other. As he reached the door, he turned round. Alissa was staring at him.

"Jack," she said, "how do you think I'll look in a tartan skirt?"

*

He knew he had not been eating. Zademe read the weight and shouted out in amazement. The reading was fifteen stone, three pounds. Zademe said the steam room would sort out the final pound.

"You look pleased with yourself," said Petra.

"Time to see your tattoo," Jack announced. "Fifteen stone and three pounds. The steam room will sort out the remaining pound."

Petra called the waiter and ordered a bottle of champagne. After it was served she held up her glass and then leaned over and kissed Jack.

"We'll call it settled," she said. "No need for the steam room." She drank deeply. "But we need to talk."

"You're backing out?" angered Jack.

"No, I'm not. I'll show you my tattoo," she said. "But I need to prepare you."

"You're embarrassed. I get that. Just lift your blouse."

"It's not that simple." She waved at the waiter who refilled their glasses.

"I won't look at your breasts, if that's the issue,"

laughed Jack.

"You won't be missing much," smiled Petra.

"Tomorrow at 7." She sipped her drink. "But please, Jack, it is not what you are expecting to see."

"What are you talking about? I've lost four stone and now it's time to show me your tattoo. What could be more straightforward?"

"If only it was that simple," said Petra.

The following day Jack worked with his new finance director, met with the investment teams, checked the progress of the implementation of their updated processes, lunched with a prospective new client and chaired two meetings in the afternoon. He continually checked his watch: he was counting down the hours.

All is revealed

Jack met another woman. He had not expected to do so but she was waiting with Petra when he arrived at the hotel. He had spoken to Alissa who was planning her trip to Scotland.

"Jack," said Petra. "This is Dr Lizzie Wellings, a friend of mine from medical school. She's a hospital doctor." She seemed to hesitate. "We're going downstairs."

Zademe had organised a private room and the three of them entered. It was well lit. Petra went into the cubicle.

"She is undressing , Jack."

"Does she need a chaperone?" he snapped.

"No, but you do," said the doctor. Petra came out wearing a white robe. She moved in the centre of the room facing away from Jack. Dr Wellings asked him to stand ten feet away from Petra and behind her. She went over to her friend and whispered in her ear. Petra nodded. She went back and stood with Jack.

Slowly, Petra disrobed. The towelling fell off her shoulders, down past her buttocks and on to the floor. Jack stared at the naked woman and went weak at the knees. Dr Wellings grabbed his hand. Petra's back was tattooed from top to bottom. And then Jack realised the truth. What was the term she had used? He whispered to the doctor.

"Mongolian Spot," he said. She nodded and squeezed his fingers.

*

From birth, Petra's back had been covered with the dark bruising known as Mongolian Spot. Her childhood had been brutal and, as she matured, she simply never revealed her body to anyone. On the night in Vietnam, she had risked going to bed with the dishy Australian and he had reacted with revulsion. She had walked the streets in dispair until she came across Saigon Ink. It took three days and two thousand US dollars. A brilliant tattooist named Binh Nguyen had used the bruising as the background to a landscape of total beauty.

At the top of her back were the clouds, white, dark and threatening thunder, covering the mountain range with paths leading down to her buttocks which formed the head of the valley. Down her one leg was a pathway by a stream and down the other was a waterfall. Throughout the whole landscape were people, climbing mountains, scaling peaks or descending down to the valley floor. Children were swimming in the water. There was flora and fauna. The sun was peeping through the clouds on the one shoulder.

*

Petra turned round, ignoring her nakedness. She reached Jack and put her arms around his neck.

"You are the first non-medical person to see my tattoo," she said.

"Cheerio, you two," said Dr. Wellings. "I've a late evening hospital shift to go to." Jack and Petra were clinging to each other and did not realise she had left.

There's always a future

"For the first time in my life I felt clean," she said. Saigon Ink had a mirror room and I spent hours in there living my tattoo as Binh allowed me to watch his design develop. When I came back to the UK, I contacted Lizzie and she arranged for a dermatologist to give me a full examination. There was a small infection on the inside of my buttock. I think Binh slipped with the needle. That was cleared up with antibiotics and I've been given the all-clear."

The pianist in the hotel lounge was playing a piece of music by Debbie Wiseman: 'Water Lily' suited their mood.

"When we met in here I was pondering how I could show my tattoo to a man." She laughed and sipped her vodka and tonic. "Along came Mr City Moneyman and he needed help. Quite a deal, Jack?" He told her about Alissa.

"Brilliant," Petra judged. "It's too horrible to imagine rape but it happens, all too frequently, but the woman must get back into real life as soon as possible. Loving mothers have no idea the damage they can do, however well-meaning they are." She sipped her drink. "Will Alissa take the job?"

"It's possible. They want her which, at the moment, seems like good therapy." He paused and drank far too much of his lager. "The worst part of the whole episode is that she had fallen in love with Hector. She told me she was looking for affection and, when he came along, she thought that was it for the rest of her life."

"We're all looking for love, Jack," said Petra. "What a shame you're married. It's back to Mrs Simpson for you."

"No more Tuesday evenings?" pleaded Jack.

"I've no room for any more tattoos," she laughed. "I'm around Jack, but let's give it a break." He finished his drink and stood up.

"Any idea how many calories there are in a pint of beer?" asked Petra.

"Don't care," he said. They came together and he looked into her face. There was no powder on the bruise and it looked wonderful. He was feeling rather flat. This was it. He had lost fifty-six pounds in weight, found the real Jack

Simpson, and lost the woman who had created his journey of transformation. She squeezed his bottom and held on briefly. They kissed but it was all over.

He left the hotel and decided to walk home, not because it was worth about six hundred calories, but because he did not really want to arrive back and sleep alone again. He had so much to do at work as new executives were recruited and he wanted to try to stay close to his children.

He spotted a beggar with one leg. He knew it was a fraud: their minders bought the pitches and made ridiculous amounts of money because British people are gullible. He decided that this person might be in need and he would start his new life by setting the standards he wanted to maintain.

He put his hand in his back pocket with the intention of giving the tramp ten pounds. Something was wrong. He stopped and went into a shop entrance. He replaced his hand in the pocket and pulled out the anticipated notes. There was something else. It was a photograph of a tattoo covering a woman's back. He thought it was the most beautiful thing he had ever seen. He turned it over and read the message:

Tuesday, Mr City Moneyman, 7.00 and don't be late. Petra x

He seemed to lose pounds in weight as he continued his walk home.

THE END

TONY DRURY'S BOOKS

Finance Houses: Their Development and Role in the Modern Financial Sector
(Waterlow Publishers: 1982)

Investment Clubs: The Low Risk Way to Stockmarket Profits
(Rushmere Wynne: 1995)

The DCI Sarah Rudd Thriller Series:
Megan's Game
The Deal
Cholesterol
A Flash of Lightning
The Lady Who Turned
I Will Find You
(City Fiction)

The Novella Nostalgia Series
Lunch With Harry
Twelve Troubled Jurors
Forever on Thursdays
The Man Who Hated
A Search for the Truth
(City Fiction)

REFERENCES

Throughout the book:"(The) Square Mile" and "The City of London" common usage: no copyright cover.

P1. 'The world is quite like London, it's not good, it's not bad, it just is.
There's no morality or dishonour, just your own lonely code, until your race is run, until the end'.
These are words from the film 'Legend' about the Kray twins. They are spoken by Ronnie Kray's widow beyond the grave. They do not appear in any copyright material.

P5. Walt Disney: 'Growing old is mandatory, but growing up is optional'
This quote appears in Wikipedia and WD's biography. Also, in words of quotes.

P5. Cesare Pavese: 'The real application of old age is remorse'.
The poet's CV and Wikipedia.

P11. Captain Mainwaring "You stupid boy" From Dad's Army. Used everywhere.

P12. Mike Tyson 'The Baddest man on the planet'. A phrase used all over boxing bibliography.
P14. Nigel Horton. "I give it, I take it." I was there when he said it!

P17. Jeremy Thorpe's CV. Taken from Wikipedia but found in many sources.

P19. Margaret Reid. Her book about the Secondary Crisis is out of print and all over the internet. She died in the 1950s.

P21. Marie Antoinette speaking before the guillotine fell. Found in many sources.

P23. American Senator; 'Phoney War'. Found in several sources and Wikipedia.

P25 onwards. 'Be Fit or be Damned' 1967. Found in many sporting libraries and out of copyright.

P29. Director. Mercantile Credit. "Do you realise Drury". Long deceased and said to me.

P30. 'The pen is mightier than the sword'.
1839: Edward Bulmer-Lytton. Commonly used in literary works.

P31. 1995 Leasing fraud case. Leonard Bartlett. Reported in many places and law papers.

P33. 'Finance Houses: Their development and role in the Modern Financial Sector. I own the copyright.

Page 35. The Fall and Rise of reginal Perrin' BBC archives and Wikipedia.

Page 37. Extensive commentary on Robert Maxwell. Many sources or personal contact. All over Wikipedia.

Page 43. Peter Jay. Various books about Maxwell, his website and personal recollection.

Page 49. Photograph of the signing of the 'Banking World' contract. I own the photograph. Everybody in the photograph is deceased – except me.

Page 53. Maxwell death. Reported extensively.

Page 54. 'Beauty is in the eye of the beholder'. From Wordsworth poem, perhaps the most quoted poem of all time.

P56. E L James. 'Fifty Shades of Grey'. Quoted everywhere.

P57. Ghislaine Maxwell. Biography and personal recollection.

P62. Fraudster: Elizabeth Anne Holmes. Reported extensively in the 'Financial Times' and personal recollection.

P69. Nadine Dorries. CV from Wikipedia and personal recollection.

P70. Baroness Moan. Internet searches and 'Daily Mail' articles.

P71. Bert Bacharach. Wikipedia and personal recollections.

P72. Margaret Thatcher. Perhaps the most written about PM of all time.

P79. ProShare/ProShare Investment Club.
Personal files and personal recollections. Extensively recorded on the internet.
The section on Emma Kane has been approved for publication by Emma Kane herself.

P85. Bryce Taylor. Personal recollection. Difficult to sources as he has disappeared. Found material on him eventually.

P90. History of the London Stock Exchange. Public information and the LSE website.

P91. AIM/PLUS Markets. You need to know where to look but actually public information.

P99. Global Financial Crisis. Many sources and media articles.
P107. Former DC David Palmer and Mohammad Miah fraud case. MM has disappeared. This section has been signed off for publication by David Palmer.

P110. All comments on 'Megan's Game'. I own the copyright. Information from Paul Tucker has been signed off by him.

P120. Boris Johnson. Part personal opinion and part media articles.

P127. Creative Support'. Personal experience and all data confirmed by their published material.

P132. The section on ZeroPA has been signed off by their CEO Saqhib Ali. I am Chairman of ZeroPA.

P138. 'Earn Your Health'. Two of the founders, Teresa Quinlan and Kathryn Bullock have helped in the preparation of this section. I own the copyright to the Healthy Future booklet.

P160. Garry Willinge. Pal in Hong Kong has signed this off.

P164. 'The Forbidden Tattoo'. Published by City Fiction. I own the copyright.

INDEX

Printed in Great Britain
by Amazon